KING OF KINGS
A BOOK ABOUT JESUS

MARK DRISCOLL
WITH GERRY BRESHEARS

King of Kings: A Book About Jesus
© 2025 by Mark Driscoll and Gerry Breshears

ISBN: 978-1-966223-11-5 (Hard cover), 978-1-966223-09-2
(Paperback), 978-1-966223-10-8 (E-book)

CONTENTS

ABOUT PASTOR MARK DRISCOLL

Pastor Mark Driscoll is a bold, unapologetic Bible teacher with a master's in theology. He is a sought-after preacher and public speaker and has authored over 60 books and study guides, including popular titles like *New Days Old Demons*, *Act Like a Man*, and *Real Romance*, which he co-wrote with his wife, Grace. Pastor Mark and Grace have served in ministry together since 1993 and have raised five kids who love and serve Jesus.

Today, Pastor Mark is the Founding and Senior Pastor of Trinity Church in Scottsdale, Arizona, where four generations of his family serve Jesus together. Having become grandparents, they love nothing more than to spend their free time being grandpa and grandma, also known as Bop-Bop and Nanna.

Pastor Mark has spent the better part of his life teaching verse-by-verse through books of the Bible, contextualizing its timeless truths and never shying away from challenging, convicting passages that speak to the heart of current cultural dilemmas.

Pastor Mark and Grace founded RealFaith together with their daughter Ashley in 2016. At RealFaith, it's all about changing lives with practical truth. From best-selling books to viral sermons to in-depth classes and videos, the Bible-based resources help hundreds of millions of people around the globe each year to deepen their faith, love their families, and leave a legacy.

If you'd like to learn more, visit **RealFaith.com** or download the **RealFaith app**. If you have any prayer requests or a testimony regarding how God has used this and other resources to help you learn God's Word, we would love to hear from you at **hello@realfaith.com**.

ABOUT DR. GERRY BRESHEARS

In addition to serving as a professor of theology at Western Seminary in Portland, Oregon since 1980, Dr. Gerry Breshears is a pastor to pastors and a member of the elder and preaching teams at Grace Community Church in Gresham, Oregon. He gets the honor of teaching and preaching in churches and seminaries across not only the United States but the world including Ukraine, Uganda, Poland, Lebanon, Russia, the Taiwan region, the Netherlands, and the Philippines. He was also a founding board member on The Bible Project.

Upon graduating from the University of New Mexico - Albuquerque in 1968, Gerry started his ministry as a junior high math teacher in Jefferson County, Colorado before God called him to the Philippines to teach at Faith Academy in 1969. After God changed the direction of his life, he did seminary (Denver Seminary, MDiv, 1975) and his Ph.D. (Fuller Theological Seminary, Ph.D., 1984) to become a missionary church planter and Bible college teacher in the Philippines. Then, God interrupted his life again and brought him to Western Seminary.

In addition to writing the original *Doctrine: What Christi*ans Should Believe book with Pastor Mark in 2010, Dr. Breshears and Pastor Mark also co-authored *Vintage Jesus* (2008), *Death by Love* (2008), and *Vintage Church* (2009). He also contributed a section called "Spiritual Abuse" to Bev Hislop's

Shepherding Women in Pain: Real Women, Real Issues, and What You Need to Know in 2020.

He and his wife Sherry have been married since 1968 and have two sons and a daughter. They enjoy collecting kids, so they have a growing number of non-legal (not illegal) children, grandchildren, and great grandchildren. Together, they enjoy ministering and extending hospitality to others.

DEDICATION FROM MARK DRISCOLL AND GERRY BRESHEARS

This book is dedicated to our kids who love and serve Jesus, in faith that our grandkids will grow up to do the same, and one day great grandkids (already present for Gerry) will continue faithful ministry to Jesus Christ in every generation until we are all together for the forever family reunion in the Kingdom of God.

DOWNLOAD THE REALFAITH APP TO GET
MORE BIBLE TEACHING FROM PASTOR
MARK & GRACE.

WANT TO BUILD YOUR FAITH?
UNLOCK A DEEPER WALK WITH JESUS
WITH A FREE DIGITAL COPY
OF PASTOR MARK'S 365-DAY DEVOTIONAL
THROUGH THE BOOK
OF ROMANS!

PREFACE

In 2007, Dr. Gerry Breshears and I released a book titled *Vintage Jesus* addressing the big questions about Jesus for that generation. The endorsements for that book included the following:

> This new book by Driscoll, one of the most promising young pastors I've met, and his theological partner Gerry Breshears, tell the old, old story in a contemporary, exciting, in-your-face manner. Though written to appeal to today's younger seekers, nothing of classic Christian theology is omitted. Those of my generation may bridle at some aspects of the book—but it's good if we do. This book is just what's needed for us to understand how to reach the postmoderns and a great tool to help all of us connect with young seekers. This is both bold and uncompromising. I can highly recommend it.
> —Chuck Colson, founder, Prison Fellowship

> This book reveals Mark Driscoll as a highly powerful, colorful, down-to-earth catechist, targeting teens and twenty-somethings with the old, old story told in modern street-cred style. And Professor Breshears ballasts a sometimes lurid but consistently vivid presentation of basic truth about the Lord Jesus Christ.
> —J. I. Packer, Board of Governors' professor of theology, Regent College

The two men who graciously provided those endorsements have since passed away, and I have gone from being a young pastor to a grandfather. Today, newer generations are asking both old and new questions about Christ, and those generations are now the ages of our children, who all are serving Jesus. Dr. Breshears, who was my seminary professor decades ago, has kindly helped me write and publish *King of Kings* for a new generation with new questions. By God's grace, perhaps in 18 more years, I will be able to write yet another book like this answering the questions of my grandkids and their peers. Thank you for giving us the honor of helping you learn about the real

Jesus in a world filled with counterfeits.

Our focus in this book is to not just look back on Jesus while He was on the earth in humility but as He is today, and as He will be when He returns – in sovereign, majestic glory for all eternity as King of Kings. We believe that as Jesus gets bigger, life becomes clearer, problems become smaller, and hope becomes deeper.

Lastly, as you read this book, the voice will largely be mine. Hopefully this makes the book easy to read and understand, which is our hope.

Pastor Mark Driscoll

CHAPTER 1
IS KING JESUS THE ONLY GOD?

"...you, being a man, make yourself God." –Jesus' enemies (John 10:33)

J esus Christ. No one is more loved and hated than Jesus Christ.

The name *Jesus* is derived from the Old Testament name Joshua, which means, "Yahweh God is salvation." The title Christ means one chosen and anointed by God to be the Messiah who delivers God's people.

Roughly 2,000 years ago, Jesus was born in a small town filled with poor and simple families. His mom, Mary, was most likely a young teenage girl, and His adoptive dad was a carpenter named Joseph. Jesus spent roughly the first 30 years of His life in obscurity, swinging a hammer with His dad.

Around the age of 30, Jesus began a public ministry that included preaching, performing miracles, caring for the suffering, casting out demons, and befriending social misfits, something controversial for a holy man. Jesus' ministry spanned only three short years before He was put to death for declaring Himself to be equal with God. He died by shameful crucifixion like tens of thousands of people before and after Him.

At first glance, Jesus' résumé is rather simple. He never traveled more than a few hundred miles from His home, never held a political office, never wrote a book, never married, never had sex, and never had an office or a desk. He died both homeless and poor.

Nonetheless, Jesus is the most famous person in human history. More songs have been sung to Him, artwork created of Him, and books written about Him than anyone who has ever lived. Jesus looms so large over human history that we measure time by Him; our calendar is divided into the years before and after his birth, noted as B.C. ("before Christ") and A.D. (anno Domini, meaning "in the year of the Lord"), respectively.

No army, nation, or person has changed human history to the degree that Jesus has. Emperor Napoleon Bonaparte, who conquered much of Europe, said, "I know men and I tell you that Jesus Christ is no mere man. Between Him and every other person in the world there is no possible term of comparison."[1]

Some 2,000 years after He walked the earth, Jesus remains as popular as ever. To begin our study of Him, we will consider various concepts about Christ.

JESUS OF CHRISTIANITY

The Bible plainly and frequently says Jesus is God. Matthew calls Jesus "'Immanuel' (which means, God with us)."[a] Thomas calls Jesus, "My Lord and my God!"[b] Romans 9:5 speaks of "the Christ who is God over all, blessed forever. Amen." Titus 2:13 refers to "our great God and Savior Jesus Christ". Titus 3:4 calls Jesus "God our Savior." 1 John 5:20 says that Jesus Christ "is the true God." Lastly, 2 Peter 3:18 speaks of "our Lord and Savior Jesus Christ."

The New Testament refers to Jesus Christ as "Lord" several hundred times.[c] That term is the equivalent of the Old Testament term "Yahweh," which is the personal name of God. Thus, this title, Lord, is ascribed to Jesus Christ as God and Lord.

In Revelation 22:13, Jesus says, "I am the Alpha and the Omega, the first and the last, the beginning and the end." With these titles, He is obviously referring to Himself as eternal God. A Bible commentator says:

> The titles refer to the sovereignty of God and Christ over history. They control the beginning of creation and its end, and therefore they control every aspect of history in between. Since this is the only passage to contain all three titles, it has the greatest emphasis of them all on the all-embracing power of Christ over human history.[2]

COUNTERFEIT CHRISTS

Sadly, every generation seeks to give Jesus an extreme makeover, all the way back to Marcion [A.D. 85-160].[3] Embarrassed by the moody, angry, violent God of the Old

---

[a] Matt. 1:23 [b] John 20:28 [c] E.g., Rom. 10:9, 13; 1 Cor. 2:8; Heb. 1:10

KING OF KINGS

Testament, along with scenes of Jesus flipping over tables and rebuking people in the New Testament, he launched a public relations campaign. He tried to eliminate the Old Testament and put a few heavy coats of varnish on the Gospels, making Jesus soft with a soothing disposition. The Bishop of Sinope, who happened to be his dad, condemned him as a heretic.

In addition to the real Jesus, there are numerous counterfeit versions of Christ. Paul promised this demonic deception in 2 Corinthians 11:3–4 saying,

> But I am afraid that as the serpent deceived Eve by his cunning, your thoughts will be led astray from a sincere and pure devotion to Christ. For if someone comes and proclaims another Jesus than the one we proclaimed, or if you receive a different spirit from the one you received, or if you accept a different gospel from the one you accepted, you put up with it readily enough.

To help you know the real Jesus, we will now examine some counterfeit versions of Christ and then return to the real Jesus.

For starters, it is foolish to claim that all religions essentially teach the same thing. When it comes to Jesus, various spiritualities, along with the cults and world religions, in no way teach the same thing and vary wildly.

Progressive woke "Christians" say Jesus was merely a good man, but not the Godman. Unitarian Universalism teaches that Jesus was not God but rather essentially an incarnation of a great man to be respected solely for His teaching, love, justice, and healing. According to Scientology, Jesus is an "implant" forced upon a thetan about a million years ago.

Various teaching streams portray Jesus as a mere man who evolved into a deity through spiritual evolution. This includes an early church heresy called adoptionism. This false teaching said that Jesus was merely a man who was given supernatural powers at the time of His baptism and later raised from death and adopted into the Godhead as the Son of God. Adoptionism sadly continues in a variety of forms. In New Spirituality (or New Age) teaching, Jesus was a man who ascended to a higher level of consciousness and became more integrated with the spiritual life force that runs through all things. As a result, He achieved a higher plane of being and divine status. New Age guru Deepak Chopra said, "I see Christ as a state of consciousness we can all aspire to."[4]

JESUS OF THE CULTS

In the most basic sense, there is a difference between a cult and a religion and how each presents Jesus Christ. A cult starts as Christian, or at least professing to be Christian, and then veers off course into false teaching that is out of line with the Scriptures and history of the Christian Church creeds. A world religion never claimed to be part of the Christian Church, and its' portrait of Jesus does not pretend to follow the teachings of the Bible.

The cult known, since 1931, as the Jehovah's Witnesses cult began with C. T. Russell as the Zion's Watch Tower Tract Society in the 1870s. They teach that Jesus Christ is the incarnation of the archangel Michael, created billions of years ago by God before other beings and then aiding in the rest of creation. Importantly, they do not see Jesus as the fully divine second person of the Trinity.[5] However, the Bible is clear that only God creates.[a] Hebrews 1:2-3 speaks of Jesus Christ as God the Father's "Son, whom he appointed the heir of all things, through whom also he created the world. He is the radiance of the glory of God and the exact imprint of his nature, and he upholds the universe by the word of his power." Colossians 1:16–17 says of Jesus Christ, "For by him all things were created, in heaven and on earth, visible and invisible, whether thrones or dominions or rulers or authorities—all things were created through him and for him. And he is before all things, and in him all things hold together." Throughout the Bible, it is clear that God is the one who creates, and Jesus Christ is that Creator God.

What makes cults particularly confusing and dangerous

---

[a] Job 9:8; Isaiah 44:24

is that they use Christian terms but have completely different meanings for them and twist the Scriptures like Satan did when he tempted Jesus. The Church of Jesus Christ of Latter-Day Saints, aka Mormons, uses the name "Jesus" but teaches that He was purely human in His life here on earth and that, because He was super obedient, He would become a god of another planet someday. One scholarly book on Mormonism summarizes their cultic and counterfeit view of Christ saying,

> The Mormon Scriptures do reference Jesus Christ as the Son of God (Helaman 5:12; 3 Nephi 14:24-6; Mosiah 3:8), and their Articles of Faith open with the assertion that Jesus Christ is the Son of God the Eternal Father. Indeed, the Mormon doctrine of God is often confusing to Christians because it uses the language that is familiar to them but means something different by it.[6]

We go on to learn,

> For Mormonism, the eternality of God means a prehuman spiritual existence followed by a period of probation in a physical body, and then evolution to a status of godhood once again. The thrust of this idea is that humankind itself is destined to become a god. The widely quoted epigram articulated by Lorenzo Snow, the fifth president of the church, captures this curious and paradoxical equation: "As man is, God once was; as God is, man may become." Numerous other statements by Mormon theologians confirm this teaching.[7]

These evolutionary concepts see humanity as moving up the spiritual ladder toward godlike status. Satan first used this temptation with Adam and Eve, saying, "you will be like God..."[a] The truth is not that we go up a ladder of good works or consciousness to godlike status but that God in Jesus Christ humbly came down to be with us.

----
[a] Gen. 3:5

Surprisingly, Mormons believe that Father God is father of all people, including Jesus. They say, "We are all literally children of God, spiritually begotten in the premortal life."[8] Thus, they say Jesus is their elder brother, along with the one who fell and became Satan.[9] This means there is, in essence, no difference between Jesus and all other humans.

Lastly, Mormons do not pray to or worship Jesus, according to Bruce McConkie, one of the Twelve Apostles of the LDS Church. He said in a talk at Brigham Young University named after the Mormon leader, "We do not worship the Son, and we do not worship the Holy Ghost."[10]

JESUS OF THE PARANORMAL

The concept of Jesus as an alien has grown increasingly popular and is the theme of a number of documentary-type shows on TV and YouTube. When we think of an alien, we tend to think of the monsters created in science rather than someone like Superman. Consider for a moment the similarities between Jesus Christ and Superman.

- Both were sent to earth by their fathers from other worlds.
- Both were raised by poor parents in rural areas.
- Neither started to publicize their powers until they were around 30 years of age.
- Both appeared to be ordinary people in every way if you simply saw them going about their business as a carpenter or news reporter, respectively.
- Both had exemplary character devoted to truth and justice.
- Both helped people in need by endangering their own lives.
- Neither married.
- Neither fathered children.
- Both brought people back from death.
- Both came back from death themselves.
- Both saved the people of earth.

Of course, Superman is fictitious, whereas Jesus actually walked the earth. If they even exist, aliens are not God, and so Jesus was not an alien, if the Bible is to be believed. Jesus was opposed and ultimately killed for repeatedly, emphatically, and publicly saying He was God, not an alien. Jesus said He came from Heaven, not another world. Mark 14:61–64 (NIV) says:

> ...the high priest asked him, "Are you the Messiah, the Son of the Blessed One?" "I am," said Jesus. "And you will see the Son of Man sitting at the right hand of the Mighty One and coming on the clouds of heaven." The high priest tore his clothes. "Why do we need any more witnesses?" he asked. "You have heard the blasphemy..."

Jesus used the divine title "Son of Man"—taken from Daniel 7, where God comes to earth as a man. When the religious leaders heard this, they rightly understood Jesus to be saying He was God who had come from Heaven to earth and not an alien visiting from another planet. Jesus suffered and died for saying He was God and never intimated that He was an alien or created being from another planet. Rather, Jesus is the Creator God who made all the planets and beings.

JESUS OF THE OCCULT

The occult mixes Christianity with dark, demonic, and deceptive spirituality. A Bible Dictionary says of the occult, "This term, meaning 'hidden,' is applied to practices which are below the surface of normal life. They may be contacts with the evil spirit world, deliberately sought through (black) magic or Satanism."[11]

Freemasonry, or the Masons, includes 14 United States presidents, 18 vice presidents, and five Supreme Court chief justices. Masonic lodge meetings include the reading of Scripture but intentionally omit the name "Jesus."[12] The pastor, Levi Dowling, who became a demonic channeler penning the blasphemous book *The Aquarian Gospel of Jesus the Christ*, said Jesus underwent seven degrees of initiation (an occultic ceremony) in Egypt, with the seventh degree making him the Christ.[13] Former Sunday School teacher Edgar Cayce, who became a channeler of the demonic as a psychic, said Jesus only became the Christ in His thirtieth incarnation after shedding His bad karma.[14] These attempts to blend Jesus with the demonic realm of the occult are an effort to create a counterfeit Christ and open people to Satanic spirituality.

JESUS OF THE RELIGIONS

Bahá'ís say that Jesus was a manifestation of God and a prophet but inferior to Muhammad and Bahá'u'lláh. Buddhism teaches that Jesus was not God but rather an enlightened man like the Buddha. Hinduism, with its many views of Jesus, does not consider Him to be the only God, but most likely a wise man or incarnation of God, much like Krishna.

The Dalai Lama, spiritual leader of Tibetan Buddhism, said, "[Jesus] was either a fully enlightened being, or a bodhisattva [a being who aids others to enlightenment] of a very high spiritual realization."[15] Indian Hindu leader Mahatma Gandhi said, "I cannot ascribe exclusive divinity to Jesus. He is as divine as Krishna or Rama or Muhammad or Zoroaster."[16]

Islam is now the second largest world religion after Christianity and on pace to rival Christianity as the dominant religious ideology on earth by 2050.[17] Islam teaches that Jesus was merely a man and a prophet who came before and was supplanted by Muhammad. Islam does not believe that Jesus died by crucifixion, is the Son of God or to be worshipped as God. One Muslim leader has even said, "If Jesus were here, he'd be a Muslim."[18]

People unfamiliar with the deep, irreconcilable differences between Christianity and Islam try to downplay this fact in the pursuit of a reconciled unity between the two, nothing that any true Muslim or Christian desires. A religious scholar says,

Some try to downplay the distinctions between Muslim and Christian belief about Christ, but this is not wise nor charitable...The tension between the two religions was enhanced by the fact that the Koran contains several references to the life of Jesus which, of course, are accepted by Muslims as absolute and indisputable truth as they constitute God's own word, while they contradict Christian dogma on certain points....The Koran acknowledges the virgin birth. Jesus is the Word which God placed into Mary. This, however, does not mean that he should be called "God's Son." Rather, he is the last great prophet before Muhammad, a healer and a model of love, poverty, and humility, who never thought of claiming divine status...But in the Koran, the crucifixion is not accepted: "They did not kill him and did not crucify him, rather one was made resembling him (Sura 4.157)." Hence, the central importance of the Cross in Christian faith is never properly understood by a Muslim, even less so the need for redemption is acknowledged, because Islam does not know the concept of original sin. According to the teaching of the modern Ahmadiyya sect, Jesus wandered to Kashmir after someone else had been crucified in his place; his tomb is taken to be near Srinagar where he died at a great age.[19]

JESUS OF GOD THE FATHER

Who exactly is Jesus? Is He a good man or God, the half-brother of Lucifer, a prophet, liar or truth-teller, therapist or communist, the only God or just one of the many gods? From beginning to end, the Bible repeatedly and clearly declares that Jesus is God.[a]

There is simply no authority higher than God the Father. God the Father said Jesus was God. In Hebrews 1:8, the Father speaks of the Son as God, saying, "But of the Son he says, 'Your throne, O God, is forever and ever.'" When Jesus is brought forth out of the water at His baptism, God the Father says in Matthew 3:17, "This is my beloved Son, with whom I am well

---

[a] Matt. 4:7; 28:9; Luke 4:12; John 1:1–4, 14; 5:17–18; 8:58; 10:30–33; 12:37–41 cf. Isa. 6:9–11; 20:28–29; Acts 20:28; Rom. 9:5; Col. 1:16–17; 2:8–9, Phil. 2:10–11; 1 Cor. 2:8; 4:4; 8:4–6; 1 Tim. 6:15; Titus 2:13; 1 John 5:20; Heb. 1:8; 2 Pet. 1:1; Rev. 1:8, 17–18; 17:14; 19:16; 22:13–16

pleased."

At Jesus' transfiguration, "a voice from the cloud said, 'This is my beloved Son, with whom I am well pleased; listen to him.'"[a] There can be no greater testimony to the deity of Jesus Christ than that of God the Father. He says Jesus is God!

JESUS OF JESUS

So much has been said about Jesus that it only seems appropriate to let Jesus speak for Himself. There are 11 ways by which Jesus plainly said He is the only God.

1. Jesus said He came down from Heaven.

On rare occasions, people will claim that they have been taken into Heaven through something like a near-death experience (NDE). Jesus, however, made the opposite claim – that He came down from Heaven, "For I have come down from heaven..."[b] His audacious claim got Him into trouble with those who heard Him and they

> ...grumbled about him, because he said, "I...came down from heaven." They said, "Is not this Jesus, the son of Joseph, whose father and mother we know? How does he now say, 'I have come down from heaven'?"...When many of his disciples heard it, they said, "This is a hard saying..." After this many of his disciples turned back and no longer walked with him.[c]

Jesus' claim to be God walking on the earth has never been made by the founder of any other world religion. The closest anyone has come is the assertion by some Hindus that the Buddha is an avatar of Vishnu. But the Buddha himself never made such a claim. Conversely, Jesus clearly stated that He is God. God alone calls Heaven His eternal home, and God alone could descend from Heaven as opposed to ascending up to

---

[a] Matt. 17:5 [b] John 6:38 [c] John 6:41-66

Heaven.

Finally, coming down from Heaven reveals Jesus' eternality as God; He existed before His birth as a man, which is the repeated teaching of the New Testament.[a]

2. Jesus said all of Scripture was about Him.

The Bible opens by telling us that it is all about God as the subject, hero, and center. Genesis 1:1 says, "In the beginning, God..." The rest of the Bible reveals who this God is. Jesus Christ came as a rabbi, or teacher, and said that He was the God of the Bible and came to fulfill everything the Scriptures said. Furthermore, there is no correct interpretation of the Bible without repentance of sin and faith in Him as the only God:

- Matthew 5:17–18 – "Do not think that I have come to abolish the Law or the Prophets; I have not come to abolish them but to fulfill them. For truly, I say to you, until heaven and earth pass away, not an iota, not a dot, will pass from the Law until all is accomplished..."
- John 5:38-40 – "...[Jesus said to religious leaders] you do not have his word abiding in you, for you do not believe the one whom he has sent. You search the Scriptures because you think that in them you have eternal life; and it is they that bear witness about me, yet you refuse to come to me that you may have life..."
- Luke 24:27, 44-45 – [After Jesus' Resurrection] beginning with Moses and all the Prophets, he interpreted to them in all the Scriptures the things concerning himself... Then he said to them, "These are my words that I spoke to you while I was still with you, that everything written about me in the Law of Moses and the Prophets and the Psalms must be fulfilled." Then he opened their minds to understand the Scriptures...

---

[a] John 1:15; 3:13; 8:58; 13:13; 17:15,24; 1 Cor. 8:6; 15:47; 2. Tim 1:9; Heb. 5:5-6; 13:8; 1 Pet. 1:20; Rev. 1:8; 13:8

While the Scriptures are for us, they are not primarily about us. Rather, they are about Jesus Christ. Practically, Jesus can be found in six ways in the Old Testament, just as He taught.

One, Old Testament prophecies point to Jesus as we will study in another chapter in this book.

Two, the old Testament appearances of the being who is called the "Angel of the Lord" and also "YHWH" are cameo appearances before He is born of Mary. For example, He speaks to Moses in the Burning Bush[a], calls Gideon to lead Israel[b], and speaks to Isaiah in the temple.[c]

Three, Old Testament institutions point to Jesus. For example, the Temple housing the presence of God points to Jesus body as God's presence on earth. When priests offer sacrifices, they point to Jesus, who is our priest and shed His blood for our sin. Jesus tabernacled among us and then identified Himself with the Temple.[d]

Four, Old Testament events point to Jesus. For example, when Sodom and Gomorrah were suddenly destroyed by fire, they point to Jesus doing the same at the judgment of His Second Coming. When Joseph was betrayed by his brothers, thrown in a hole left for dead, and later came out to rule and reign at the right hand of the King of Egypt, he was a type of Jesus who would do the same by getting out of the grave following His betrayal to rule from the right hand of the Father of the Kingdom of God. When Moses delivered God's people from evil and slavery in the Exodus, he was pointing to the coming of Jesus as the greater liberator. When Jonah was in the fish for three days and came out to preach salvation to a nation, he was pointing to Jesus who would spend three days in a grave and came forth to preach salvation to every nation. Finally, holy days like Passover pointed to "Christ, our Passover lamb" who was "sacrificed" so that death for sin would pass over us.[e]

Five, Old Testament titles point to Jesus. Examples include First and Last[f], Light[g], Rock[h], Husband or Bridegroom[i],

------

[a] Exodus 3:14 [b] Exodus 3:14 [c] Isa. 6:1-8; John 12:38-41 [d] John 1:14; 2:18-22 [e] 1 Corinthians 5:7 [f] Isa. 41:4; 44:6; 48:12 cf. Rev. 1:17; 2:8; 22:13 [g] cf. Rev. 1:17; 2:8; 22:13 Ps. 27:1 cf. John 1:9 [h] Pss. 18:2; 95:1 cf. 1 Cor. 10:4; 1 Pet. 2:6–8 [i] Hos. 2:16; Isa. 62:5 cf. Eph. 5:28–33; Rev. 21:2

Shepherd[a], Redeemer[b], Savior[c], and Lord of Glory[d].

Six, Old Testament representative figures point to Jesus. For example, the priests point to Jesus as our Great High Priest, kings point to Jesus as King of Kings, sages point to Jesus whose wisdom is "greater than Solomon"[e], judges point to Jesus as the Judge of the living and the dead, shepherds point to Jesus as our Good Shepherd, and prophets like Moses point to Jesus as the literal Word of God and greatest Prophet.

3. Jesus said He was more than just a good man.

Many people think Jesus was a good man but not God. Thich Nhat Hanh, author of *Living Buddha, Living Christ* and considered by many to be the most respected interpreter of Buddhism to the western world after the Dalai Lama, said of Jesus, "Of course Christ is unique. But who is not unique? Socrates, Muhammad, the Buddha, you, and I are all unique."[20]

The idea that Jesus was good but not God is nothing new. Mark 10:17–18 says, "And as he was setting out on his journey, a man ran up and knelt before him and asked him, 'Good Teacher, what must I do to inherit eternal life?' And Jesus said to him, 'Why do you call me good? No one is good except God alone.'" This man likely thought he was honoring Jesus by calling him a "good teacher." However, Jesus replied that since everyone is a sinner, there is no such thing as a good person— God is the only good person. In saying this, Jesus was revealing to the man that He was not merely a good person, but in fact God. Even Jesus' enemies were equally clear that Jesus refused to be considered merely a good man. They wanted to kill Jesus because he was "making himself equal with God."[f]

This fact of Jesus' uniqueness as more than just a good spiritual man is incredibly important. Perhaps the legendary Billy Graham said it best: "Jesus was not just another great religious teacher, nor was he only another in a long line of individuals seeking after spiritual truth. He was, instead, truth

---

[a] Ps. 23:1 cf. Heb. 13:20 [b] Hos.13:14; Ps. 130:7 cf. Titus 2:14; Rev. 5:9 [c] Isa. 43:3 cf. John 4:42 [d] Isa. 43:3 cf. John 4:42 [e] Matthew 12:42 [f] John 5:18

itself. He was God incarnate."[21]

4. Jesus said He is the Son of Man.

When picking a title for Himself, Jesus was most fond of "Son of Man," applying it to Himself in about 30 different events. The title comes from Daniel 7, penned more than 500 years before Jesus' birth. In Daniel's vision, this most enigmatic human figure comes with the clouds to be presented to the Ancient of Days, the Lord Himself. There, He is given messianic dominion and authority, something no angel can obtain. Then all nations worship Him! Psalms 110 sees this divine person sitting alongside the Lord as an equal. This second person of the Trinity was promised to receive the messianic mission to redeem the world and rescue sinners. As God, He is exalted over all peoples, nations, cultures, and religions to be worshiped as the eternal King. Jesus is the one who claimed to be the Son of Man coming on the clouds as God.[a]

5. Jesus performed miracles.

Jesus was a great leader and teacher, but His ministry also included the miraculous—one line of evidence that He was, in fact, God and more than just another spiritually enlightened person. In contrast, Unitarian Universalism says,

> Most of us would agree that the important thing about Jesus is not his supposed miraculous birth or the claim that he was resurrected from death, but rather how he lived. The power of his love, the penetrating simplicity of his teachings, and the force of his example of service on behalf of the disenfranchised and downtrodden are what is crucial.[22]

However, Jesus is emphatic that He did perform miracles,

---

[a] Matt. 24:30; 26:64; Mark 13:26; 14:62-64; Luke 21:27; 22:69; Acts 1:9-11; 1 Thess. 4:17; Rev. 1:7; 14:14

and they helped prove His claims that He is God. In John 10:36b–39, Jesus said,

> "...do you say of him whom the Father consecrated and sent into the world, 'You are blaspheming,' because I said, 'I am the Son of God'? If I am not doing the works of my Father, then do not believe me; but if I do them, even though you do not believe me, believe the works, that you may know and understand that the Father is in me and I am in the Father." Again they sought to arrest him, but he escaped from their hands.

We will examine Jesus' miracles in more detail, but John 20:30–31 connects Jesus miracles and divinity saying, "Now Jesus did many other signs in the presence of the disciples, which are not written in this book; but these are written so that you may believe that Jesus is the Christ, the Son of God, and that by believing you may have life in his name."

6. Jesus said He is God.

Jesus clearly, emphatically, and repeatedly said He is God. If His statements were untrue, it would have been a blasphemous violation of the first commandment. The belief that Jesus is God is not something that Christians made up but rather something that Christians believe because it was taught by Jesus Himself. Many cults wrongly deny that Jesus is God or ever claimed to be God. For example, the Jehovah's Witnesses Watchtower Society says, "Jesus never claimed to be God."[23]

Christian Science founder Mary Baker Eddy flatly states, "Jesus Christ is not God."[24]

Jesus clearly said He is God, and His hearers clearly understood His unparalleled claim. Mark 14:61–64 reports that, under oath on trial,

> ...the high priest asked him, "Are you the Christ, the Son of the Blessed?" And Jesus said, "I am, and you will see the Son of Man seated at the right hand of Power, and coming

with the clouds of heaven." And the high priest tore his garments and said, "What further witnesses do we need? You have heard his blasphemy. What is your decision?"

John 8:58–59 reports that Jesus said, "'Truly, truly, I say to you, before Abraham was, I am.' So they picked up stones to throw at him, but Jesus hid himself and went out of the temple."

Jesus claimed divine eternality in saying that He existed before Abraham, who lived roughly 2,000 years prior. In naming Himself "I am," Jesus was declaring Himself to be the same God who revealed Himself by the title "I am" some 1,400 years prior, speaking to Moses through the burning bush.[a] Those who heard Jesus rightly understood Him as declaring Himself to be the eternal God who saved Abraham and called Moses. Consequently, they called him a blasphemer for being a man who claimed to be God and sought to kill Him for it.

In John 10:30–33, Jesus said,

"...I and the Father are one." The[y] picked up stones again to stone him. Jesus answered them, "I have shown you many good works from the Father; for which of them are you going to stone me?" The[y]...answered him, "It is not for a good work that we are going to stone you but for blasphemy, because you, being a man, make yourself God."

Throughout history, numerous people have claimed to speak for God. Yet there is a surprisingly short list of people who have actually claimed to be God. Religious leaders such as Buddha, Krishna, Muhammad, and Gandhi did not claim to be God. In fact, they assured their followers that they were not God. Jesus, in contrast, clearly and repeatedly said He is God. This is simply an astonishing claim that people kept seeking to kill Jesus for saying, because it would clearly be blasphemy if untrue. Jesus was not killed for His good deeds or clever parables, but rather because He claimed to be God.

New York Judge Gaynor said of Jesus' trial at the end of his

---

[a] Exodus 3:14

earthly life, "It is plain from each of the gospel narratives, that the alleged crime for which Jesus was tried and convicted was blasphemy."[25]

7. Jesus confirmed to others He is God.

Not only did Jesus repeatedly declare that He is God, but He also reiterated this fact when others doubted or opposed that claim. Matthew 26:63–65 says of Jesus when He was on trial:

> ...the high priest said to him, "I adjure you by the living God, tell us if you are the Christ, the Son of God." Jesus said to him, "You have said so. But I tell you, from now on you will see the Son of Man seated at the right hand of Power and coming on the clouds of heaven." Then the high priest tore his robes and said, "He has uttered blasphemy. What further witnesses do we need? You have now heard his blasphemy."

Religious leaders sought to condemn Jesus publicly for committing blasphemy (declaring himself to be God). The penalty for blasphemy was death. If Jesus were not claiming to be God but instead misunderstood, we would expect Him to clarify the misunderstanding to avoid a bloody death. But it was no mistake—Jesus declared He is God. Lastly, the Scriptures testify to additional occasions in which the religious leaders in Jesus' day recognized His claim to be God, for which Jesus never did apologize or recant.[a]

8. Jesus said He was sinless.

Sins of omission are when we fail to do something good, and sins of commission are when we do something wrong. Sin includes our thoughts, motives, words, and deeds, which are all seen objectively by an all-knowing God. Throughout history,

---

[a] Matt. 26:63-65; John 5:17-23; 8:58-59; 10:30-39; 19:7

no one has claimed with any credibility that they are without sin, because it would mean their words, actions, thoughts, and motivations are continually perfect and pure. As the old adage goes, no one is perfect.

Religious leaders praised for their moral uprightness, such as Mohammad, Gandhi, Mother Teresa, and Billy Graham, have acknowledged their own sinfulness. As we read the Gospel accounts of Jesus' life, we often see Him calling others to repent. We also see Jesus being tempted to sin.[a] Nevertheless, nowhere does Jesus sin or repent of any personal sin, because He was without sin. Jesus' enemies sought to bring up false charges of sin against Jesus, but their lies never agreed with one another and were found to be groundless.[b]

Jesus declared that He was not only morally superior to everyone who has ever lived but, in fact, sinless. He further challenged anyone to prove Him wrong, saying, "Which one of you convicts me of sin? If I tell the truth, why do you not believe me?"[c]

The perfect, sinless life of Jesus makes Him admittedly more holy and worthy of our devotion than anyone who has ever lived, and it helps to prove that He was and is God because God alone is without sin. Jesus' disciples, most of whom suffered and died without recanting, repeat this claim throughout the New Testament, making it unparalleled in history.[d] Even a hardened Roman centurion, akin to a Nazi Storm Trooper, said, "Certainly this man [Jesus] was innocent!"[e] Jesus was perfect in that He never sinned, even when He was being tempted and tortured beyond imagination.

Those who testify to the sinlessness of Jesus are those who knew Him most intimately, such as his friends Peter[f] and John[g], His half-brother, James[h], and even His former enemy Paul.[i] Additionally, even Judas, who betrayed Jesus, admitted that Jesus was without sin[j], along with the ruler Pilate who oversaw the murder of Jesus[k], a soldier who participated in the murder of Jesus[l], and the guilty sinner who was crucified at Jesus' side.[m]

---

[a] For example, Luke 4 [b] Mark 14:55-56 [c] John 8:46 [d] Isa 53:9; John 8:46; 2 Cor 5:21; Heb 4:15; 7:26; 1 Pet 1:19; 1 John 3:5 [e] Luke 23:47 [f] Acts 3:14; 1 Pet. 1:19; 2:22; 3:18 [g] John said that anyone who claims to be without sin is a liar (1 John 1:8) and also said that Jesus was without sin (1 John 3:5) [h] James 5:6 [i] 2 Cor. 5:21 [j] Matt. 27:3-4 [k] Luke 23:22 [l] Luke 23:47 [m] Luke 23:41

9. Jesus forgave sin.

While many of the resources in our world are spent on dealing with the effects of sin (e.g., war, illness, death, depression, crime, and poverty), there is still no way apart from Jesus for people to have their sins forgiven. At best, some religions teach their adherents what they can do to work hard at paying God back through such things as good works and reincarnation; they still lack any concept of forgiveness.

In light of this, Jesus' claims to forgive sin are simply astonishing. Speaking to a sinful but repentant woman, Luke 7:48 reports, "And [Jesus] said to her, 'Your sins are forgiven.'" Luke 5:20–21 also says, "And when [Jesus] saw their faith, he said, 'Man, your sins are forgiven you.' And the scribes and the Pharisees began to question, saying, 'Who is this who speaks blasphemies? Who can forgive sins but God alone?'" Their incredulous response is exactly correct: while we can forgive sins against us, only God can forgive sins committed toward another person.

Sin is the human problem. All sin is ultimately committed against God.[a] Subsequently, God alone has the power to forgive the sins of sinners.[b] Jesus could only forgive sin because He was and is God. In making this claim, Jesus is inviting us to confess our sins to Him so that we may be forgiven through His substitutionary death and bodily resurrection. If He were not God, our sin simply could not be forgiven by Him and He would be a false teacher.

10. Jesus taught people to pray to Him and worship Him as God.

Prayer is how we talk to God. Jesus Christ repeatedly taught us to pray to Him.[c] Doing so, Jesus was clearly stating that He is God. As a result of His teaching, women like the Canaanite[d] and men like Stephen did pray to Jesus as God. In Acts 7:59, at the moment of his painful death by stoning,

---

[a] Ps. 51:4 [b] Jer 31:34; Ps 130:4 [c] John 14:13-14; 15:16; 16:24 [d] Matt. 15:25

Stephen prayed, "Lord Jesus, receive my spirit." Multitudes throughout history and a few billion worshipers of Jesus on the earth today have, like Stephen, cried out to Jesus in prayer. If Jesus is not God or powerful enough to answer our prayers, then He is a cruel sadist for teaching us to pray to Him in faith.

Jesus also welcomed people to worship Him as God. The Bible is emphatically clear that only God is to be worshiped.[a] To worship anyone other than God is both idolatry and blasphemy—two sins that the Bible abhors from beginning to end with the strongest condemnations.

Worshipers of Jesus include the magi[b], blind man[c], previously demonized man[d], Thomas the doubter[e], His best friend John[f], all of the disciples[g], a group of women[h], the mother of James and John[i], angels[j], entire churches[k], His own mother[l] and half-brothers[m], little children[n], and even His former enemies such as Paul.[o] Jesus repeatedly accepted the worship of people throughout the course of His life without rebuking or correcting them.

Jesus also said that He is to be worshiped along with God the Father: "...all may honor the Son, just as they honor the Father. Whoever does not honor the Son does not honor the Father who sent him."[p] Upon His triumphal entry into Jerusalem, when children worshiped Him, Jesus quoted Psalm 8:2 in reference to Himself as God to be worshiped:

> But when the chief priests and the scribes saw the wonderful things that he did, and the children crying out in the temple, "Hosanna to the Son of David!" they were indignant, and they said to him, "Do you hear what these are saying?" And Jesus said to them, "Yes; have you never read, 'Out of the mouth of infants and nursing babies you have prepared praise'?"[q]

Commenting on this event, a Bible scholar says, "Jesus' response, again using the introductory rebuke 'Have you never

---

[a] Deut. 6:13; 10:20; Matt. 4:10; Acts 10:25–26 [b] Matt 2:11 [c] John 9:38 [d] Mark 5:6 [e] John 20:28 [f] Isa 6:1-5 cf. John 12:41; Rev 1:17-18 [g] Matt 14:33; 28:17 [h] Matt 28:8-9 [i] Matt 20:20 [j] Heb 1:6 [k] 1 Cor 1:2 [l] Acts 1:14 [m] Acts 1:14; James; Jude [n] Matt 21:14-16 cf Ps 8:2 [o] Rom 9:5; Col 1:15; 2:9; Titus 2:13 [p] John 5:23 [q] Matt. 21:15–16

read?' tacitly applauds their acclamation in light of Ps 8:2…
There the children are praising Yahweh, so Jesus again accepts
worship that is reserved for God alone."[26]

Furthermore, Philippians 2:10–11 envisions a day in which
everyone bends their knee in subjection to Jesus and lifts their
voice in worship of Jesus as Lord. Taken together, all of this
evidence reveals that Jesus was and is God.

11. Jesus said He is the only way to Heaven.

Not only did Jesus declare that He came down from
Heaven, but He also taught that He alone is the only way for
anyone else to enter into Heaven. While many religious and
spiritual teachers claim to lead to Heaven, they do not claim to
be that path themselves. Jesus, in contrast, said in John 14:6,
"I am the way, and the truth, and the life. No one comes to the
Father except through me."

Some will protest that other religions provide additional
paths to Heaven, but Jesus debunked those myths by declaring
that He alone is the sole, narrow path to eternal "life" and
that all other paths are merely paths to eternal "destruction."[a]
Sadly, even some pastors do not believe in Christ. One female
Episcopalian bishop was asked by *Time* magazine, "Is belief in
Jesus the only way to get to heaven?" Grossly, she contradicted
Jesus, saying, "We who practice the Christian tradition
understand him as our vehicle to the divine. But for us to
assume that God could not act in other ways is, I think, to put
God in an awfully small box."[27]

The bedrock of Christianity is that Jesus Christ is the
incarnation of only God. This has been the foundational
commitment of the Christian Church since the beginning.
Archaeologists continue to uncover the lands of the Bible. Over
and over, the Scriptures are proven true. Recently, researchers
discovered an ancient mosaic declaring Jesus as God.

The earliest inscription declaring Jesus as God - deemed

---

[a] Matt 7:13-14

"the greatest discovery since the Dead Sea Scrolls" - was uncovered beneath the floor of an Israeli prison and is now on display...The 1,800-year-old mosaic, discovered by an inmate of the Megiddo prison, features the ancient Greek writing: "The god-loving Akeptous has offered the table to God Jesus Christ as a memorial." The 581-square-foot mosaic decorated the world's first prayer hall in 230 AD, confirming Christians believed Jesus was the son of God from the very beginning...The floor has been hidden under the prison since it was discovered in 2005, but has now been lent to a museum in Washington, DC... Carlos Campo, CEO of the museum, hailed the mosaic as "the greatest discovery since the Dead Sea Scrolls," while his colleagues noted it was "the most important archaeological discovery for understanding the early Christian church."[28]

The question remains to be answered: how should we respond to the incredible person, work, and claims of Jesus after considering these 11 reasons to believe Jesus is the only God? Only three possible responses remain: Jesus was a lunatic, Jesus was a liar, or Jesus is Lord. British author C. S. Lewis said:

A man who was merely a man and said the sort of things Jesus said would not be a great moral teacher. He would either be a lunatic—on the level with the man who says he is a poached egg—or else he would be the Devil of Hell. You must make your choice. Either this man was, and is, the Son of God; or else a madman or something worse. You can shut Him up for a fool, you can spit at Him and kill Him as a demon; or you can fall at His feet and call Him Lord and God. But let us not come with any patronizing nonsense about His being a great human teacher. He has not left that open to us. He did not intend to.[29]

Liar?

If untrue, Jesus' claims to be God would make Him an

evil cult leader much like David Koresh, who had a lengthy, televised standoff with law enforcement. Upwards of 85 of his followers died in their Waco compound, including approximately 25 children. Only nine members of the cult survived. Koresh proclaimed himself the "Son of God" and said he and not Jesus was the Lamb of Revelation.[30] Koresh was quoted as saying, "Do you know who I am? God in the flesh . . . stand in awe and know that I am God."[31] If Jesus is not God but claimed to be God and deceived others into dying for that claim, He is the worst man who has ever lived.

Lunatic?

Sadly, some people have mental health problems that keeps them from dealing with reality. These people need professional help and rather than being given a public platform should be encouraged to live a more private life supported by those who love them. If Jesus Christ was not God but said He was the eternal Creator who came down from Heaven, should be prayed to and worshiped, and would rise from the dead to open Heaven, then He would have mental illness. The academic journal *Psychological Reports* article, "The Messiah-Complex in Schizophrenia" explains that people who think they are the messiah have mental illness and a form of schizophrenia that requires professional help to manage if they are to have a functional life.[32]

To state the obvious, if Jesus is not God, but wrongly thought He was, we should have compassion for Him but not be committed to Him.

Lord?

The truth is that Jesus is not a liar or a lunatic but rather God our Lord. The appropriate response to Jesus is turning from sin to worship Him alone. According to the first two commandments[a], there is only one God, and that God alone is

---

[a] Ex. 20:1-6

to be worshiped. The one God to be worshiped is Jesus Christ.

Having surveyed both what is said about Jesus by others and by Jesus Himself, His own question to us is a fitting conclusion to this chapter: "But who do you say that I am?"[a] Have you personally trusted in Jesus Christ as your only God and Savior? If not, we would encourage you to become a Christian right now in prayer, which is simply talking to God. You can simply say to God, "I acknowledge that I am a sinner. I believe that Jesus is my God and Savior. I invite Jesus to forgive my sin, and commit to follow Him as my God." If you prayed that prayer, please let a Christian friend or family member know and contact us at **hello@realfaith.com** so we can pray for you and get you started on reading the Bible for yourself.

---

[a] Matt 16:15

CHAPTER 2

HOW HUMAN WAS KING JESUS?

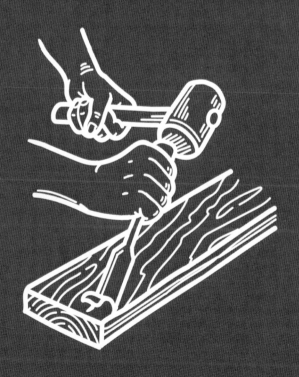

"Behold, the virgin shall conceive and bear a son, and they shall call his name Immanuel" (which means, God with us). – Matthew 1:23

J esus was a dude. Like my drywaller dad, He was a construction worker who built things for a living.[a] Because Jesus worked in a day when there were no power tools, He likely had calluses on His hands and muscles on His frame and did not look like so many of the images that portray Him with long, flowing, feathered hair, perfect teeth, and soft skin. No, Jesus was a man everyone would automatically respect.

The truth is that we have no idea how Jesus looked because there is simply no historical evidence. The Byzantines put a beard on Jesus as a symbol of power. The Victorians made Jesus' blond. Out of the more than 50 mainstream films made about Jesus, He has never been played by an actor who is ethnically Jewish, which means those portrayals are also likely inaccurate.[33]

If we had seen Jesus walking around before His baptism, we would have seen a normal guy heading off to work. He did the normal things that actual people do, like eating meals and brushing His teeth. Entire books of the Bible (such as 1 John) are written in large part to defend that Jesus was fully human with a real physical body that functioned like our physical bodies. In sum, Jesus looked like a normal, average dude as one Bible translation says, "He sprouted up like a twig before God, like a root out of parched soil; he had no stately form or majesty that might catch our attention, no special appearance that we should want to follow him."[b]

JESUS WAS FULLY MAN

The Bible affirms the humanity of Jesus Christ in numerous ways. Jesus had a human name—Jesus (meaning "Yahweh saves") Christ (meaning "anointed one")—and a human genealogy.[c] He was born of a woman[d], had brothers

---

[a] Mark 6:3 [b] Isa 53:2, NET Bible [c] Matt. 1:1–17; Luke 3:23–38 [d] Matt. 1:18–25; Luke 2:7; Gal. 4:4

and sisters[a], and was racially Jewish.[b] Jesus grew physically, spiritually, mentally, and socially[c], learned[d], experienced fatigue[e], slept[f], grew hungry[g] and thirsty[h], worked a job[i], had male and female friends[j], gave encouraging compliments[k], loved children[l], celebrated holidays[m], went to parties[n], loved His mom[o], prayed[p], worshiped[q], and obeyed God the Father.[r]

Furthermore, not only did Jesus have a physical body[s], but He also suffered and died "in the flesh."[t] In addition to His body, Jesus also had a human spirit.[u] Jesus also experienced grief[v], had compassion[w], was stressed[x], astonished[y], happy[z], told jokes[aa], and even wept.[bb]

Taken together, these are clearly the ways we speak of human beings and reveal that Jesus was a man.[cc] 1 John 4:2–3 says,

> By this you know the Spirit of God: every spirit that confesses that Jesus Christ has come in the flesh is from God, and every spirit that does not confess Jesus is not from God. This is the spirit of the antichrist, which you heard was coming and now is in the world already.

The belief in the full humanity of Jesus Christ was the dominant position of the early Christian church. The church father Athanasius (293-373 A.D.) said:

> Peter writes in his letter, "Christ therefore suffered in the flesh for our sakes" [1 Pet. 4:1]. So when it is said that he hungered and thirsted and toiled and was ignorant and slept and cried out and made requests and fled and was born and turned away from the cup—in general, did all the things which belonged to the flesh—let...all things of this sort be asserted as "for our sakes in the flesh,"

---

[a] Matt. 13:55 [b] John 4:9 [c] Luke 2:42, 52; 3:23 [d] Matt. 4:12; Mark 11:13–14; Luke 2:40, 5 [e] Matt. 8:24; Mark 4:38; Luke 8:23–24; John 4:7 [f] Mark 4:36–41 [g] Matt. 4:2; Mark 11:12; Luke 4:2 [h] John 4:7; 19:18 [i] Mark 6:3 [j] John 11:3–5 [k] Mark 12:41–44 [l] Matt. 19:13–15 [m] Luke 2:41 [n] Matt. 11:19 [o] John 19:26–27 [p] Matt. 14:23; Mark 1:35; 14:32–42; John 17 [q] Luke 4:16 [r] John 5:30; 6:38; 8:28–29, 54; 10:17–18 [s] Rom. 8:3; Phil. 2:7–8; Heb. 2:14; 1 John 4:2–3 [t] Rom. 8:3; Eph. 2:15–16; Col. 1:21–22; Heb. 2:14; 10:19–20; 1 Pet. 2:24 [u] John 12:27; 13:21; 19:30 [v] Matt. 23:37; Luke 19:41 [w] Matt. 9:36; Mark 1:41; Luke 7:13 [x] John 13:21 [y] Mark 6:6; Luke 7:9 [z] Luke 10:21–24; John 15:11; 17:13; Heb. 12:2, 22 [aa] Matt. 7:6; 23:24; Mark 4:21 [bb] John 11:34–35 [cc] John 8:40; Acts 17:31; 1 Tim. 2:5

for this is precisely the reason the apostle himself said, "Christ therefore suffered" not in the Godhead but "for our sakes in the flesh," in order that the passions might be recognized to be natural properties not of the Logos but of the flesh.[34]

WHAT DOES INCARNATION MEAN?

Incarnation (from the Latin meaning "becoming flesh") is the word Bible scholars use to explain how the second member of the Trinity entered into human history in flesh as the God-man Jesus Christ. A theological journal explains that the English word "incarnation" comes from the root word carn- ("flesh"), literally meaning that Jesus Christ is God who came in flesh.[35] A Bible Dictionary says,

> incarnation is a theological assertion that in Jesus the eternal Word of God appeared in human form (Jn 1). Many theologians picture the incarnation as the voluntary and humble act of the second person of the Trinity, God the Son, in taking upon himself full humanity and living a truly human life. The orthodox doctrine of the incarnation asserts that in taking humanity upon himself, Christ did not experience a loss of his divine nature in any way but continued to be fully God.[36]

Jesus' incarnation is clear in John 1:14: "And the Word became flesh and dwelt among us, and we have seen his glory, glory as of the only Son from the Father, full of grace and truth." To better understand the incarnation, we must carefully consider the entire opening chapter of John's Gospel.

In the Hebrew Old Testament, the Word of God was the presence and action of God breaking into human history with unparalleled power and authority. God's Word indicated action, an agent accomplishing the will of God. God brings things into existence by His word[a] and God's word is sent out

---

[a] Gen. 1:3, 6, 9, 11, 14, 20, 24; Ps. 33:6

to accomplish His purposes.[a] For the Hebrew, God's speech and action were one in the same.

Heraclitus, also known as the "weeping philosopher," was at the fountainhead of Greek philosophy. Popular, his image remained on the coins in Ephesus for several centuries following his death. For Heraclitus, the creation of the world, the ordering of all life, and the immortality of the human soul were all made possible solely by the word (or logos) that was the invisible and intelligent force behind this world. It was the word through which all things were interrelated and brought into harmony. The key to all wisdom and understanding was a deep and clear awareness of one thing—the Word, or *logos*.

Jesus Christ was born at a time and place in which the Hebrew and Greek worlds collided. In this context, John wrote his biography of Jesus in the Greek language and began with the concept of "the word," a common ground in both Hebrew theology and Greek philosophy. Logos is from the Greek meaning "word" or "reason."

John begins with a declaration that both Hebrews and Greeks would have agreed with, that before the creation of the world and time, the Word existed eternally. He then boldly says Jesus is the Word and was with the one and only God and, in fact, was Himself God and was face-to-face with God the Father from eternity.[b]

John then teaches that the Word is not merely the invisible, impersonal force of the Greeks. He fulfills what is hinted in the Old Testament[c] that the Logos is a Person through whom all things were created[d], and a Person in whom is life and light for mankind.[e] This light that exposes sin and reveals God has come into the darkness of this sinful, cursed, and dying world. The darkness opposed His light but was unable to understand or overcome Him.[f]

It is important to note that John was fully monotheistic, believing only in one God.[37] John was Jesus' best friend, and this was a massive statement he could be killed for. John understood the magnitude of what he was saying, and, as a

---

[a] Isa. 55:11 [b] John 1:1–2 [c] Psa. 33:6, 45:6-11 [d] John 1:3; cf. Col. 1:16 [e] John 1:4 [f] John 1:5; cf. 1 John 1:5–10; 2:8–11

result, he very clearly outlined his position. John was acutely aware of and intentional in his revolutionary teaching regarding five aspects of this Logos.

1. *The Logos is eternal.*[a] A Bible scholar says, "'In the beginning'...refers to a point in eternity past beyond which it is impossible for us to go. Moreover, the verb was ('in the beginning was the Word') is an imperfect tense in the Greek, indicating continued existence."[38]

2. *The Logos has always been with God, face-to-face with the Father as an equal in relationship.*[b]

3. *The Logos is a person distinct from, yet equal to, God.*[c] The Greek preposition pros (translated "with" in 1 John 1:1 and 1:2) implies two distinct persons. Therefore, while the Father and the Logos are not the same, they do belong together as one.

4. *The Logos is the Creator*[d] *and therefore eternal, self-existent, and all-powerful.*

5. *The Logos became flesh.*[e] John clearly taught that matter is not inherently evil, and that God does involve Himself with the material. Jesus came to dwell among His people in a way that is similar to the tabernacle that God had the Israelites build as His sanctuary so that He might dwell in their midst.[f] As a Bible scholar says, the Logos became flesh to reveal to humans five things: life[g], light[h], grace[i], truth[j], glory[k], and even God Himself[l].[39]

John repeats this theme in his other writings. 1 John 1:1 says he and others heard, saw, and touched the Logos, "which was from the beginning..." This is a clear reference to Jesus Christ. Revelation 19:12–13 also pictures Christ as the conquering warrior, the Logos of God.

In summary, the Logos is one of the strongest arguments for the deity of Jesus Christ as the personal, eternally existing Creator of the universe, distinct from yet equal with God the

---

[a] John 1:1–2 [b] John 1:1–2 [c] John 1:1–2 [d] John 1:3 [e] John 1:14 [f] Ex. 25:8 [g] John 1:4 [h] 1 John 1:4–5 [i] John 1:14 [j] Ibid. [k] Ibid. [l] John 1:18

Father, who became incarnate (or came in flesh) to demonstrate His glory in grace and truth to reveal life and light to men.

HOW DID GOD COME INTO HUMAN HISTORY?

Before we examine how the incarnation occurred, we will note some important truths about this doctrine for the sake of precision.

First, Jesus' incarnation is not an idea borrowed from pagan mythology. There are stories such as Zeus begetting Hercules and Apollo begetting Ion and Pythagoras. Some have speculated that Christians stole the virgin birth story from such myths. This speculation must be rejected on three grounds. (1) Some such myths came after the prophecy of Isaiah 7:14 and therefore could not have been the origination of the story. (2) The myths speak of gods having sex with women, which is not what the virgin birth account entails. (3) The myths do not involve actual human beings like Mary and Jesus but rather fictional characters similar to our modern-day superheroes in the comics.

For example, an account of the "virgin birth" of Augustus was told in the days when Jesus was born.

> When Atia had come in the middle of the night to the solemn service of Apollo, she had her litter set down in the temple and fell asleep, while the rest of the matrons also slept. On a sudden a serpent glided up to her and shortly went away. When she awoke, she purified herself, as if after the embraces of her husband, and at once there appeared on her body a mark in colors like a serpent, and she could never get rid of it; so that presently she ceased ever to go to the public baths. In the tenth month after that Augustus was born and was therefore regarded as the son of Apollo.[40]

This account wildly differs from God's miraculous working in the womb of Mary to beget the Godman, Jesus, who is Immanuel the Messiah.

Second, the Mormon teaching that God the Father had

physical, flesh-and-bone relations with Mary, thereby enabling her to conceive Jesus, is horrendously incorrect, as we will prove in chapter 4.

Third, the incarnation does not teach that a man became God. From the time the Serpent told our parents, "...you will be like God,"[a] there has been an ongoing demonic false teaching that we can be gods (e.g., Mormonism) or part of God (e.g., pantheism, panentheism, and New Ageism). The incarnation teaches the exact opposite, namely that God became a man.

Fourth, the second member of the Trinity did not come into existence at the incarnation of Jesus Christ. Rather, the eternal Son of God became the God-man Jesus Christ. A noted Bible scholar says:

> The doctrine of the incarnation at once tells us that that is not what happened. A person, we repeat, did not come into being there. This person was the eternal Person, the second Person in the Trinity. When a husband and a wife come together and a child is born a new person, a new personality, comes into being. That did not happen in the incarnation.[41]

Fifth, while it is true in one sense that God did become a man, we must be careful to note that the second divine person in the Trinity became a man and that the entire Trinity did not incarnate as a human being. Therefore, by incarnation, we mean that the eternal second person of the Trinity entered into history as the man Jesus Christ, not God the Father or God the Holy Spirit.

The incarnation of Jesus Christ is recorded in detail in the first two chapters of both Matthew's and Luke's Gospels. We read that the angel Gabriel was sent as a messenger from God to the town of Nazareth to a young virgin named Mary, who was betrothed to a man named Joseph.

The Church has always taught the virgin motherhood of Mary. A religious scholar says that apart from a few very minor

---

[a] Gen. 3:5

false teachers, "...nobody of Christians in early times is known to have existed who did not accept as part of their faith the birth of Jesus from the Virgin Mary."[42]

There are two general ways in which various minds have erred regarding the humanity and divinity of Jesus. The first is to deny the full divinity of Jesus in favor of his humanity; the second is to deny the full humanity of Jesus in favor of his divinity.

The denial of the full divinity of Jesus has been done by heretics such as the Unitarians, social justice "Christians" who downplay or deny Jesus as God, cults including the Jehovah's Witnesses and Mormons, along with the blasphemous book and movie *The Da Vinci Code*, among others including the Ebionites, Dynamic Monarchianists, Nestorians, modalists, monarchianists, Sabellianists, Unitarians, Social Gospel proponents, "death of God" theologians, liberals, Arians, Jehovah's Witnesses, Mormons, functionalists, Adoptionists, Kenotics, and Apollinarians. According to the Jehovah's Witnesses cult, Jesus was created by God the Father billions of years ago as the archangel Michael and is not God equal to the Father.[43]

The Mormon cult teaches that Jesus was born as the first and greatest spirit-child of the Heavenly Father and Heavenly Mother and is also the spirit-brother of Lucifer, who became a god but whose deity is no more unique than many people's. Some New Agers say Jesus was not fully God and fully man but rather half man and half alien. Oneness Pentecostals falsely teach that there is no Trinity but rather that Jesus appears in the roles of Father, Son, and Spirit.

The denial of the full humanity of Jesus has been done by numerous heretics, including the New Age teaching that Jesus is a state of non-physical consciousness, among others, including the Docetists, Gnostics, Modal Monarchians, Apollinarian Paulicians, Monophysitists, New Agers, and Eutychians.

As a general rule, conservative Christians are more likely to emphasize Jesus as God. Conversely, liberal Christians are more likely to emphasize Jesus as a man. This tension became all the more public when films started to be made about Jesus Christ.

THE STRUGGLE TO PORTRAY JESUS AS BOTH GOD AND MAN

The History Channel's documentary *The Passion: Religion and the Movies* explored the fascinating relationship between the divinity and humanity of Jesus and how that has played out in the cinema. The tension between Jesus' divinity and humanity has plagued filmmakers who have made films about Him. Such films are important because they influence how people perceive Jesus. Essentially, every film about Jesus done prior to the radical 1960s emphasized the deity of Jesus.

Seven of the first 10 reel movies were about Jesus and had the word "passion" in the title. 1912 saw the first feature-length movie of Jesus, *From the Manger to the Cross.*

Legendary director and devout Christian Cecil B. DeMille transformed movie special effects with his 1923 film *The Ten Commandments.* In 1927, he produced a film about Jesus' life in the movie *King of Kings.* He carefully portrayed Jesus as very pious with little humanity, including a glowing aura, appearing like an icon. Because the film was a silent movie, the printed dialogue was changed into various languages and shown to audiences around the world. In his biography, DeMille said that 800 million people in total were introduced to Jesus through his film and that only the Bible had done more for the cause of Jesus.[44]

In 1932, Cecil B. DeMille directed the first "talkie" film based on the Bible, which stressed the humanity of Jesus. *The Sign of the Cross* explored the persecution of Christians under Nero and contained some very risqué scenes for that time. In the 1950s, *The Robe* film was released, based on the novel written by the minister Lloyd Douglas. The story centers on a Roman who helped oversee the crucifixion of Jesus and later converted to Christianity. The groundbreaking film was the first to be filmed in CinemaScope and received four Academy Award nominations.

In 1964, *The Gospel According to St. Matthew* was filmed by gay, atheist Marxist poet Pier Paolo Pasolini. He was previously imprisoned for blasphemy in connection with another film he made. Many critics consider this film to be the greatest ever made about Jesus because of the daring portrayal of his humanity. For dialogue, the film simply used every word from the Gospel of Matthew. In the spirit of the 1960s, Jesus was portrayed as a revolutionary for the poor and a social activist. To play Jesus, Pasolini chose a young student who came knocking on his door raising money for the Communist Party. No one in the film, including the young man who played Jesus, had any acting experience. The earthy film, with an emphasis on Jesus as a real human being, stood in contrast to the sweeping biblical epics of the previous era.

Pasolini's film paved the way for additional movies with an emphasis on Jesus' humanity. In 1965, director George Stevens produced *The Greatest Story Ever Told*, a three-hour film on the life of Jesus.

Godspell, the first film featuring a singing Jesus, emerged during the height of the 1970s disco craze. In 1973, the Norman Jewison film *Jesus Christ Superstar*, based on the Broadway play of the same name, was a rock opera complete with Jesus' hippie followers singing and dancing. Judas had an enormous afro and flared pants as the film made every effort to update the humanity of Jesus for the culture of the day.

In 1977, one of the most respected films about Jesus ever produced debuted on television as the miniseries *Jesus of Nazareth*. The miniseries was commissioned by the Pope, who used his 1977 Easter address to encourage people to watch it. The show was incredibly popular and was used as a missionary tool by many Christians and churches because it clearly showed both Jesus' humanity and His divinity.

In 1979, *The Jesus Film*, which told the story of the Gospel of Luke, was released, becoming the most watched movie in history. Not funded by Hollywood, the low-budget film, shown as a missionary tool in numerous nations, is claimed to have converted millions to Christianity. It strikes a balance between the humanity and divinity of Jesus.

1979 also saw the making of one of the most controversial films about Jesus. The blasphemous British *Monty Python* film titled *Jesus Christ: Lust for Glory* and later re-titled to *Life of*

Brian openly mocked Christians. In its most controversial scene, Jesus cheerily sings about always looking on the bright side of life while hanging on the cross. Churches protested the film, and it was banned in numerous cities.

Keeping with the theme of controversial films about Jesus, in 1988, director Martin Scorsese released *The Last Temptation of Christ*, which the Vatican blacklisted. In the movie, Jesus is not considered to be the Messiah but rather a man who avoids the cross and lives a normal human life, which included marriage. This film about Jesus was so controversial that no other Bible film would be made in Hollywood for the next decade.

Then, Mel Gibson's film *The Passion of the Christ* exploded upon the world in 2004, grossing over $600 million at the box office alone. It is the highest-grossing R-rated movie ever. In its first week, it debuted at number one, despite its graphic violence. The success of the film is due, in part, to its ability to show the humanity of Jesus through the pain of His flogging and crucifixion, without in any way negating His deity.

THE EMOTIONAL LIFE OF JESUS CHRIST

Listening to most Christian music stations, you'd get the impression that Jesus was always mild-mannered, endlessly patient, open, affirming, tolerant, only spoke in kind words, never got angry, and ran from conflict. The former major league baseball player turned evangelist Billy Sunday was closer to the truth saying, "Jesus was the greatest scrapper who ever lived."[45]

Bible scholars have struggled with the emotions of God in general and Jesus in particular. One theologian reports, "The Thirty-Nine Articles of the Church of England and the Westminster Confession of Faith described God as 'without body, parts, or passions.'"[46]

Perhaps this misconception explains the prevalence of passionless Christianity: If God is "without ... passions," then our relationship with Him should also be one that is dispassionate and without emotions. Part of the Holy Spirit's ministry in the life of Jesus was directing His emotions, including joy. Luke 10:21 (NIV) reveals, "Jesus, full of joy through the Holy Spirit ..." The emotional life of Jesus' disciples is later reported in Acts 13:52, which says, "the disciples were filled with joy and with the Holy Spirit."

A Bible scholar says, "Unfortunately, contemporary evangelicals have paid little attention to the development of a theology or biblical anthropology of the emotions, affections, and feelings."[47]

To help correct this error, we will examine the emotional life of Jesus Christ. First, the Old Testament predicted the emotional life of Jesus Christ. For instance, Isaiah 53:3–11 promised Jesus would be despised, rejected, a man of sorrows, acquainted with grief, stricken, smitten, afflicted, crushed, oppressed, and have anguish in His soul.

A book about Jesus' emotions says, "Jesus is seldom thought of in emotional terms."[48] We will now examine each mention of Jesus' emotions in the four Gospels, including compassion, which is the most common.

Jesus' emotions in Matthew

Here are the mentions of Jesus' emotions in Matthew's Gospel in the English Standard Version (ESV) translation of the Bible, with some other translations included to help provide a richer and fuller understanding:

- 8:10 – "marveled" (ESV, NASB, NKJV), "amazed" (NIV, HCSB, NLT)
- 9:30 – "sternly warned"
- 9:36, 14:14, 15:32 – "compassion"
- 20:34 – "pity" (ESV), "compassion" (HCSB, NASB, NKJV, NIV), "felt sorry for them" (NLT)
- 26:37–38 – "sorrowful and troubled", "My soul is very sorrowful, even to death."
- 27:46 – "Jesus cried out with a loud voice, saying ... 'My God, my God, why have you forsaken me?'"

Jesus' emotions in Mark
A Bible scholar says,

> No Gospel writer allows us to gaze more deeply into Jesus' soul than Mark. If a psychological analysis of Jesus' personality were possible, this would be the place to begin. Mark captures a wider range of Jesus' emotions than any other Gospel. To describe the variety of Jesus' emotional reactions he uses fourteen different expressions, compared with seven in Matthew and five in Luke. ... Although there are twenty-eight references to Jesus' emotions in John (compared with sixteen in Mark), only nine different words are used.[49]

I've provided the following list of Jesus' emotions in Mark, with various translations included that give hue and color to His emotional life:

- 1:41 – "pity" (ESV), "compassion" (HCSB, NASB, NKJV, NLT), "indignant" (NIV)
- 3:5 – "anger, grieved" (ESV, NASB, NKJV), "anger and sorrow" (HCSB), "anger and, deeply distressed" (NIV) or "angrily ... deeply saddened" (NLT)
- 6:6 – "marveled" (ESV, NKJV), "amazed" (HCSB, NIV, NLT), "wondered" (NASB)
- 6:34, 8:2, 9:22 – "compassion"
- 7:34 – "He sighed" (ESV, NLT, NKJV); "He sighed deeply" (HCSB); "deep sigh" (NASB, NIV)
- 8:12 – "sighed deeply in his spirit"
- 10:21 – "loved" (ESV), "felt a love" (NASB), "with love" (NIV), "genuine love" (NLT)
- 14:33–34 – "greatly distressed and troubled ... 'My soul is very sorrowful, even to death.'"
- 15:34 – "Jesus cried with a loud voice ... 'My God, my God, why have you forsaken me?'"

Jesus' emotions in Luke
Although Luke is the longest of the four Gospels, it has the

fewest references to Jesus' emotions.[50]

- 7:9 – "marveled" (ESV, NASB, NKJV), "amazed" (HCSB, NIV, NLT)
- 7:13 – "compassion" (ESV, NKJV, HCSB, NASB), "his heart went out to her" (NIV), "his heart overflowed with compassion" (NLT)
- 10:21 – "rejoiced in the Holy Spirit" (ESV), "full of joy through the Holy Spirit" (NIV), "filled with the joy of the Holy Spirit" (NLT)
- 12:50 – "Great is my distress" (ESV); "what constraint I am under" (NIV); "how distressed I am" (NKJV); "I am under a heavy burden" (NLT)
- 19:41 – "He wept."
- 22:44 – "in agony" (ESV, NASB, NKJV), "in anguish" (HCSB, NIV), "in such agony of spirit" (NLT)

Jesus' emotions in John
A Bible scholar says,

> Of the sixty specific references to the emotions of Jesus in the Gospels, twenty-eight are found in John. ... Although the Fourth Gospel refers to the emotions of Jesus more often than each of the others, the range of emotions it records is comparatively modest. The most frequent references are to Jesus' love (18x).[a] Three times it says that he is troubled, twice that he is deeply moved, and once that he rejoices and sheds tears. There are also two references to his joy and one to his zeal. This represents a total of only six different emotions.[51]

Among the disciples, John likely had the closest relationship with Jesus as "the one whom Jesus loved." His reporting of Jesus' emotional life includes:

- 2:17 – "zeal" (ESV, HCSB, NASB, NIV, NKJV),

----

[a] Luke has eighty-six such references, John seventy-seven, Mark fifty-one, and Matthew forty-seven.

"passion" (NLT)
- 11:3, 5 – "love ... loved"
- 11:15 – "I am glad."
- 11:33 – "deeply moved in his spirit and greatly troubled" (ESV), "angry in His spirit and deeply moved" (HCSB), "groaned in the spirit and was troubled" (NKJV), "a deep anger welled up within him, and he was deeply troubled" (NLT)
- 11:38 – "deeply moved again" (ESV), "angry in Himself again" (HCSB), "deeply moved within" (NASB), "again groaning in Himself" (NKJV)
- 12:27 – "Now is my soul troubled."
- 13:1 – "He loved."
- 13:21 – "troubled in his spirit" (ESV), "deeply troubled" (NLT)
- 13:34 – "I have loved you."
- 14:21 – "I will love him."
- 15:9–12 – "I loved you ... my joy ... I have loved you."

Christians have always confessed that Jesus is the only perfect person who has or will walk the earth. His life is the portrait of what healthy humanity is supposed to be. You simply cannot be healthy or like Jesus without a healthy emotional life guided by the Holy Spirit.

JESUS SUFFERED

In all four Gospels, Jesus' emotions hit their climax at the cross. This odyssey begins in the Garden of Gethsemane, which Luke, the medical doctor, reports in Luke 22:44, "...being in agony he prayed more earnestly; and his sweat became like great drops of blood falling down to the ground." Jesus emotional anxiety caused, "perspiration in large drops like blood, or possibly hematidrosis, the actual mingling of blood and sweat as in cases of extreme anguish, strain or sensitivity."[52]

Hebrews 5:7 summarizes this moment: "In the days of his flesh, Jesus offered up prayers and supplications, with loud cries and tears..." Mark 14:33 says Jesus was "greatly distressed and troubled." Luke 22:43 says Jesus was so weary that "there appeared to him an angel from heaven, strengthening him." In anguish, Jesus prays in Luke 22:42: "Father, if you are willing, remove this cup from me." Jesus is dreading what is coming. The prophets speak of this cup as drinking the full strength of the wrath of God.[a] Knowing He is going to drink this cup for us, Jesus wrestles until finally surrendering to the Father's plan in Luke 22:42: "Nevertheless, not my will, but yours, be done."

JESUS WAS FUNNY

Perhaps the most overlooked aspect of Jesus' personality is His humor. Writing in *The Humor of Christ*, former Stanford and Harvard chaplain Elton Trueblood says:

There are numerous passages ... which are practically incomprehensible when regarded as sober prose, but which are luminous once we become liberated from the gratuitous assumption that Christ never joked. ... Once we realize that Christ was not always engaged in pious talk, we have made an enormous step on the road to understanding.[53]

He goes on to say:

Christ laughed, and ... He expected others to laugh. ... A misguided piety has made us fear that acceptance of His obvious wit and humor would somehow be mildly blasphemous or sacrilegious. Religion, we think, is serious business, and serious business is incompatible with banter.[54]

Other scholars say, "If there is a single person within the pages of the Bible that we can consider to be a humorist, it is without a doubt Jesus. ... Jesus was a master of wordplay, irony, and satire, often with an element of humor intermixed."[55] There

---

[a] Ezekiel 23:33; Isaiah 51:17; Jeremiah 25:15

are 30 humorous passages of Jesus just in the four Gospels.[56]

Scholars say, "The most characteristic form of Jesus' humor was the preposterous exaggeration."[57]

Examples include (1) pointing out the speck of sawdust in someone else's eye while overlooking the huge wooden beam in your own, and (2) the fact that you simply cannot shove a camel through the eye of a sewing needle no matter how hard you pull from the front and push from the rear.

The Gospels depict Jesus as fun due to His invitations to numerous parties with eccentric individuals and the large crowds that gathered around Him. Jesus' humor was often biting and intentionally jaw-dropping, particularly when directed at godless religious leaders. Jesus called them a bag of snakes[a], said their moms slept with the Devil[b], and mocked them for tithing out of their spice racks[c], praying like mindless fools in public[d], and sucking their faces in when they were fasting to look more holy.[e]

Self-righteous religious folks take themselves way too seriously. Jesus' response was to make fun of them. It is a prophetic function to not take religious, legalistic, smug, and self-righteous people seriously. This explains why Jesus does not make fun of hurting, suffering, and repentant people, but does publicly lampoon ungodly religious leaders who do not take Him seriously but take themselves way too seriously. Jesus has incredible wit and perfect comedic timing.

HOW COULD GOD BECOME A MAN?

In A.D. 451, the Council of Chalcedon met to wrestle with the confusion that surrounded the divinity and humanity of Jesus. They issued the Chalcedonian Creed, which cleared up many heresies that wrongly defined the humanity and divinity of Jesus. In sum, the creed declared that Jesus Christ is one person with two natures (human and divine) who is both fully God and fully man.

Theologically, the term for the union of both natures in

---

[a] Matt 23:33 [b] John 8:44 [c] Luke 11:42 [d] Matt 6:5 [e] Matthew 6:16-18

Jesus Christ is hypostatic union, which is taken from the Greek word hypostasis for "person." We summarize the hypostatic union by noting the following three facts: (1) Christ has two distinct natures: humanity and deity; (2) there is no mixture or intermingling of the two natures; (3) although He has two natures, Christ is one person. The Chalcedonian summary of the incarnation is the position held by all of Christendom, including Orthodox, Catholic, and Protestant Christians. In keeping with the biblical position of Chalcedon, we must retain both the full divinity and full humanity of Jesus Christ. To accomplish this, we must conclude that when Jesus became a man, He did not change His identity as God but rather changed His role. According to Augustine [A.D. 354-430], "Christ added to himself which he was not, he did not lose what he was."[58]

Some Bible scholars would say that Jesus retained all of His divine attributes while on the earth, embracing the seeming contradiction of affirming that He is both omniscient and does not know the date of His Second Coming. Many other theologians capture this humble emptying Himself of the divine equality, the divine lifestyle, with the phrase *he laid aside the exercise of his incommunicable divine attributes*. Some say He gave up *independent use of* His divine attributes while on earth. He got His supernatural knowledge by accessing His omniscience but only when directed to do so by the Father or the Holy Spirit. Others would say He *gave up use of* His incommunicable attributes almost all the time (perhaps with the exception of things like the transfiguration) living as a perfectly Spirit-filled human on mission of the Messiah. He got supernatural knowledge from the Holy Spirit, not from His omniscience. In any case, what this means is that Jesus did not continually use the attributes unique to deity such as His omniscience, omnipresence, or immortality while on the earth. We lean toward the final view, affirming that Jesus, in His humble state really does not know the date of the Second Coming[a], is not present when Lazarus[b], and dies.[c] He did

---

[a] Matt. 24:36 [b] John 11:6, 21, 32 [c] Matt. 27:50; Phil. 2:8

supernatural works like raising the dead[a], and healing diseases and casting out demons[b] by the power of the Holy Spirit.[c]

Jesus, who was fully equal with God in every way and the very form of God, did not see that as something to keep in His grip but emptied Himself of that equal status and role to humbly take the status and role of humanity. Philippians 2:5–11 says:

> Christ Jesus, who, though he was in the form of God, did not count equality with God a thing to be grasped, but emptied himself, by taking the form of a servant, being born in the likeness of men. And being found in human form, he humbled himself by becoming obedient to the point of death, even death on a cross. Therefore God has highly exalted him and bestowed on him the name that is above every name, so that at the name of Jesus every knee should bow, in heaven and on earth and under the earth, and every tongue confess that Jesus Christ is Lord, to the glory of God the Father.

Jesus "emptied himself," means that Jesus set aside His rights as God and the rightful continual use of His unshared divine attributes in total humility. The eternal Son of God chose to become human and live by the power of the Holy Spirit. This does not mean that Jesus in any way ceased to be fully God but rather that He chose not to avail Himself of His divine rights and those attributes unique to deity while on the earth. Thus, He lived as we must live—by the enabling power of God the Holy Spirit. We want to be clear: Jesus remained fully man and fully God during His incarnation, and He maintained all of His divine personhood and attributes, though He humbly emptied Himself of use of those unique to deity.

In this regard, Jesus was not the same as Clark Kent. Superman had special powers that other people did not have, but he lived in disguise as Clark Kent, pretending to be like the rest of us when in fact he was not.[59] Jesus is not like that. Jesus

---

[a] John 11:39-41; Mark 5:35-4 [b] Matt. 4:23-24; 8:16-33 [c] Matt. 12:28

was not pretending to be a humble, homeless, hated peasant who was faking His suffering, learning, and tempting. When the Bible said Jesus was hungry, tired, wept, bled, and died, it was in His full humanity without an ounce of fakery. Hebrews 2:17–18 says,

> …he had to be made like his brothers in every respect, so that he might become a merciful and faithful high priest in the service of God, to make propitiation for the sins of the people. For because he himself has suffered when tempted, he is able to help those who are being tempted.

Perhaps an admittedly imperfect analogy will help to clarify this difficult point. When our kids were little, I would get down on the floor to wrestle with them. Now that we're grandfathers, we do the same with our wonderful grandkids. Because we love them, want to identify with them, and be with them, we humble ourselves and lay aside some of our rights and strengths; we get down on the ground and take a beating from our grandsons like we did their dads years ago. In a similar way, the teaching of Philippians and the repeated referrals to Jesus as a servant in Scripture (especially in Isaiah and the Gospels) denote the humility of Jesus to stoop to our level and dwell with us.

CHAPTER 3
HOW DID PEOPLE KNOW KING JESUS WAS COMING?

"...everything written about me in the Law of Moses and the Prophets and the Psalms must be fulfilled." –Jesus (Luke 24:44)

When you are driving on a long road trip, it's always helpful to pay attention to the road signs. The intentional messaging helps you know you are going in the right direction and getting closer to your destination.

The Old Testament is a bit of a spiritual road trip. The ultimate goal was to see the Messiah enter into human history to glorify God by saving sinners and bringing the Kingdom by inaugurating the New Covenant. This road trip, however, would be a long one – nearly 2,000 years from Abraham to Jesus.

To keep His people moving forward in faith, God sent a series of prophets and prophecies as signs pointing forward to the coming of Christ. Jesus' entrance into history was eagerly awaited for over a millennium through prophecy. We live in a unique time in world history, with the privilege of seeing God's Word proven true.

Roughly a quarter of the Bible was prophetic at the time it was written. Many of those prophecies specifically pointed to the coming of Jesus Christ as the Messiah, the "anointed one."

Jesus Himself repeatedly said that He was the thread that wove together the entire Old Testament. Practically, this means that Scripture is not rightly understood or taught unless it is presented as a unified story leading to Jesus.[a] In this chapter, we will follow the instruction and example of Jesus by examining 25 Old Testament prophetic promises given hundreds and thousands of years before their fulfillment in Jesus.

Each prophecy reveals how God precisely prepared His people for the coming of Jesus. By connecting each promise to its corresponding fulfillment, we can see that the New Testament is built upon the Old Testament. Additionally, there are more than 300 quotes and thousands of references and inferences to the Old Testament in the New Testament.

Most of this chapter will simply be the reading of Scripture. We are trusting God the Holy Spirit, who inspired

---

[a] Matt 5:17-18; John 5:36-40; John 5:39-47; Luke 24:27, 44-45

the writing of Scripture, to also illuminate your understanding so that your trust in both Scripture and Jesus are increased. One final note: the authors listed are those credited in the Bible. The dates are approximate but accurate according to timelines taught by scholars who honor God's Word.

1. 4000 B.C.: Adam and Eve receive the prophecy that the Messiah (Jesus) would be born of a woman.

Promise: "...I will put enmity between you and the woman, and between your offspring and her offspring; he shall bruise your head, and you shall bruise his heel." (Gen. 3:15)

Fulfillment: "...when the fullness of time had come, God sent forth his Son, born of woman, born under the law..." (Gal. 4:4)

2. 2000 B.C.: Abraham receives the promise that the Messiah (Jesus) would descend from Abraham, through his son Isaac (not Ishmael), Isaac's son Jacob (not Esau), and Jacob's son Judah (not any of the other 11 brothers).

Promise: "...in you [Abraham] all the families of the earth shall be blessed." (Gen. 12:3); "God said... 'Sarah your wife shall bear you a son, and you shall call his name Isaac. I will establish my covenant with him as an everlasting covenant for his offspring after him...'" (Gen. 17:19); "I see him, but not now; I behold him, but not near: a star shall come out of Jacob, and a scepter shall rise out of Israel..." (Num. 24:17); "The scepter shall not depart from Judah, nor the ruler's staff from between his feet, until tribute comes to him; and to him shall be the obedience of the peoples." (Gen. 49:10)

Fulfillment: "...the genealogy of Jesus Christ, the son of David, the son of Abraham. Abraham was the father of Isaac, and Isaac the father of Jacob, and Jacob the father of Judah and his brothers..." (Matt. 1:1–2)

3. 700 B.C.: Isaiah prophesies that Jesus' mother would be

a virgin who conceived by a miracle and that Jesus would be God who became a man.

Promise: "Therefore the Lord himself will give you a sign. Behold, the virgin shall conceive and bear a son, and shall call his name Immanuel." (Isa. 7:14)

Fulfillment: "Now the birth of Jesus Christ took place in this way. When his mother Mary had been betrothed to Joseph, before they came together she was found to be with child from the Holy Spirit. And her husband Joseph... [was visited by] an angel of the Lord...in a dream, saying, 'Joseph, son of David, do not fear to take Mary as your wife, for that which is conceived in her is from the Holy Spirit. She will bear a son, and you shall call his name Jesus, for he will save his people from their sins.' All this took place to fulfill what the Lord had spoken by the prophet: 'Behold, the virgin shall conceive and bear a son, and they shall call his name Immanuel' (which means, God with us)." (Matt. 1:18–23)

4. 700 B.C.: Micah prophesies that Jesus would be born in the town of Bethlehem.

Promise: "But you, O Bethlehem Ephrathah, who are too little to be among the clans of Judah, from you shall come forth for me one who is to be ruler in Israel, whose coming forth is from of old, from ancient days [eternity]." (Mic. 5:2)

Fulfillment: "In those days a decree went out from Caesar Augustus that all the world should be registered...Joseph... went up from Galilee, from the town of Nazareth, to Judea, to the city of David, which is called Bethlehem, because he was of the house and lineage of David, to be registered with Mary, his betrothed, who was with child. And while they were there, the time came for her to give birth. And she gave birth to her firstborn son and wrapped him in swaddling cloths..." (Luke 2:1–7)

5. 700 B.C.: Isaiah prophesies that Jesus would live His life without committing any sins.

Promise: "…he had done no violence, and there was no deceit in his mouth." (Isa. 53:9)

Fulfillment: "For to this you have been called, because Christ also suffered for you, leaving you an example, so that you might follow in his steps. He committed no sin, neither was deceit found in his mouth." (1 Pet. 2:21–22)

6. 700 B.C.: Hosea prophesies that Jesus' family would flee as refugees to Egypt to save His young life.

Promise: "When Israel was a child, I loved him, and out of Egypt I called my son." (Hos. 11:1)

Fulfillment: "…behold, an angel of the Lord appeared to Joseph in a dream and said, 'Rise, take the child and his mother, and flee to Egypt, and remain there until I tell you, for Herod is about to search for the child, to destroy him.' And he rose and took the child and his mother by night and departed to Egypt and remained there until the death of Herod. This was to fulfill what the Lord had spoken by the prophet, 'Out of Egypt I called my son.'" (Matt. 2:13–15).

7. 400 B.C.: Malachi prophesies that Jesus would enter the temple. After the temple's destruction in A.D. 70, it no longer exists, making it impossible to fulfill the prophecy any time after that date.

Promise: "Behold, I send my messenger, and he will prepare the way before me. And the Lord whom you seek will suddenly come to his temple; and the messenger of the covenant in whom you delight, behold, he is coming, says the Lord of hosts…" (Mal. 3:1)

Fulfillment: "Now there was a man in Jerusalem, whose name was Simeon, and this man was righteous and devout, waiting for the consolation of Israel, and the Holy Spirit was upon him. And it had been revealed to him by the Holy Spirit that he would not see death before he had seen the Lord's Christ. And he came in the Spirit into the temple, and...the parents brought in the child Jesus, to do for him according to the custom of the Law..." (Luke 2:25–27)

8. 700 B.C.: Isaiah prophesies that John the Baptizer would prepare the way for Jesus.

Promise: "A voice cries: 'In the wilderness prepare the way of the Lord; make straight in the desert a highway for our God.'" (Isa. 40:3)

Fulfillment: "In those days John the Baptist came preaching in the wilderness of Judea, 'Repent, for the kingdom of heaven is at hand.' For this is he who was spoken of by the prophet Isaiah when he said, 'The voice of one crying in the wilderness: "Prepare the way of the Lord; make his paths straight."'" (Matt. 3:1–3)

9. 700 B.C.: Isaiah prophesies that Jesus would perform many miracles.

Promise: "Then the eyes of the blind shall be opened, and the ears of the deaf unstopped; then shall the lame man leap like a deer, and the tongue of the mute sing for joy." (Isa. 35:5–6)

Fulfillment: "Now when John heard in prison about the deeds of the Christ, he sent word by his disciples and said to him, 'Are you the one who is to come, or shall we look for another?' And Jesus answered them, 'Go and tell John what you hear and see: the blind receive their sight and the lame walk, lepers are cleansed and the deaf hear, and the dead are raised up, and the poor have good news preached to them.'" (Matt. 11:2–5)

10. 500 B.C.: Zechariah prophesies that Jesus would ride into

Jerusalem on a donkey.

Promise: "Rejoice greatly, O daughter of Zion! Shout aloud, O daughter of Jerusalem! Behold, your king is coming to you; righteous and having salvation is he, humble and mounted on a donkey, on a colt, the foal of a donkey." (Zech. 9:9)

Fulfillment: "And when he had said these things, he went on ahead, going up to Jerusalem…And they brought [the colt] to Jesus, and throwing their cloaks on the colt, they set Jesus on it. And as he rode along, they spread their cloaks on the road. As he was drawing near— already on the way down the Mount of Olives—the whole multitude of his disciples began to rejoice and praise God with a loud voice for all the mighty works that they had seen, saying, 'Blessed is the King who comes in the name of the Lord! Peace in heaven and glory in the highest!'" (Luke 19:28, 35–38)

11. 1000 B.C.: David prophesies that Jesus would be betrayed by a friend.

Promise: "Even my close friend in whom I trusted, who ate my bread, has lifted his heel against me." (Ps. 41:9)

Fulfillment: "And [Judas] came up to Jesus at once and said, 'Greetings, Rabbi!' And he kissed him. Jesus said to him, 'Friend, do what you came to do.'" (Matt. 26:49–50)

12. 500 B.C.: Zechariah prophesies that Jesus' betraying friend would be paid 30 pieces of silver for handing Him over to the authorities and that the payment would be thrown in the temple in disgust (again, the temple was destroyed in A.D. 70, so this prophecy could not have been fulfilled after that time).

Promise: "Then I said to them, 'If it seems good to you, give me my wages; but if not, keep them.' And they weighed out as my wages thirty pieces of silver. Then the Lord said to me, 'Throw it to the potter'—the lordly price at which I was priced by them. So I took the thirty pieces of silver and threw them into the house of the Lord, to the potter." (Zech. 11:12–13)

Fulfillment: "Then one of the twelve, whose name was Judas Iscariot, went to the chief priests and said, 'What will you give me if I deliver him over to you?' And they paid him thirty pieces of silver." (Matt. 26:14–15); "And throwing down the pieces of silver into the temple, he departed, and he went and hanged himself. But the chief priests, taking the pieces of silver, said, 'It is not lawful to put them into the treasury, since it is blood money.' So they took counsel and bought with them the potter's field as a burial place for strangers." (Matt. 27:5–7)

13. 700 B.C.: Isaiah prophesies that Jesus would be beaten, have His beard plucked out, and be mocked and spit on.

Promise: "I gave my back to those who strike, and my cheeks to those who pull out the beard; I hid not my face from disgrace and spitting." (Isa. 50:6).

Fulfillment: "Then they spit in his face and struck him. And some slapped him..." (Matt. 26:67)

14. 1000 B.C.: David prophesies that lots would be cast for Jesus' clothing.

Promise: "...they divide my garments among them, and for my clothing they cast lots." (Ps. 22:18).

Fulfillment: "When the soldiers had crucified Jesus, they took his garments and divided them... But the tunic was seamless, woven in one piece from top to bottom, so they said to one another, 'Let us not tear it, but cast lots for it to see whose it shall be.' This was to fulfill the Scripture which says, 'They divided my garments among them, and for my clothing they cast lots.' So the soldiers did these things..." (John 19:23–24)

15. 700 B.C.: Isaiah prophesies that Jesus would be hated and

rejected.

Promise: "He was despised and rejected by men; a man of sorrows, and acquainted with grief; and as one from whom men hide their faces he was despised, and we esteemed him not." (Isa. 53:3)

Fulfillment: "And those who passed by derided him…So also the chief priests, with the scribes and elders, mocked him…And the robbers who were crucified with him also reviled him in the same way." (Matt. 27:39–44)

16. 700 B.C.: Isaiah prophesies that, though hated and rejected, Jesus would not defend Himself.

Promise: "He was oppressed, and he was afflicted, yet he opened not his mouth; like a lamb that is led to the slaughter, and like a sheep that before its shearers is silent, so he opened not his mouth." (Isa. 53:7)

Fulfillment: "But when he was accused by the chief priests and elders, he gave no answer." (Matt. 27:12)

17. 1000 B.C.: David prophesies that Jesus would be crucified (hundreds of years before the invention of crucifixion).

Promise: "For dogs encompass me; a company of evildoers encircles me; they have pierced my hands and feet…" (Ps. 22:16)

Fulfillment: "And when they came to the place that is called The Skull, there they crucified him, and the criminals, one on his right and one on his left." (Luke 23:33)

18. 700 B.C.: Isaiah prophesies that Jesus would be killed alongside sinners.

Promise: "Therefore I will divide him a portion with the

many, and he shall divide the spoil with the strong, because he poured out his soul to death, and was numbered with the transgressors..." (Isa. 53:12)

Fulfillment: "Then two robbers were crucified with him, one on the right and one on the left." (Matt. 27:38)

19. 1400 B.C.: Moses prophesies that none of Jesus' bones would be broken. 1000 B.C.: David prophesies the same.

Promise: "...you shall not break any of [the Passover lamb's] bones." (Ex. 12:46); "He keeps all his bones; not one of them is broken." (Ps. 34:20)

Fulfillment: "So the soldiers came and broke the legs of the first, and of the other who had been crucified with him. But when they came to Jesus and saw that he was already dead, they did not break his legs. But one of the soldiers pierced his side with a spear, and at once there came out blood and water. He who saw it has borne witness—his testimony is true, and he knows that he is telling the truth—that you also may believe. For these things took place that the Scripture might be fulfilled: 'Not one of his bones will be broken.'" (John 19:32–36)

20. 1000 B.C.: David prophesies that Jesus would be forsaken by God.

Promise: "My God, my God, why have you forsaken me? Why are you so far from saving me, from the words of my groaning?" (Ps. 22:1)

Fulfillment: "And about the ninth hour Jesus cried out with a loud voice, saying, 'Eli, Eli, lema sabachthani?' that is, 'My God, my God, why have you forsaken me?'" (Matt. 27:46)

21. 700 B.C.: Isaiah prophesies that Jesus would die.

Promise: "...he was cut off out of the land of the living, stricken for the transgression of my people?" (Isa. 53:8b)

Fulfillment: "Then Jesus, calling out with a loud voice, said, 'Father, into your hands I commit my spirit!' And having said this he breathed his last." (Luke 23:46)

22. 700 B.C.: Isaiah prophesies that Jesus would be buried in a tomb given to Him by a rich man.

Promise: "And they made his grave with the wicked and with a rich man in his death, although he had done no violence, and there was no deceit in his mouth." (Isa. 53:9)

Fulfillment: "When it was evening, there came a rich man from Arimathea, named Joseph, who also was a disciple of Jesus. He went to Pilate and asked for the body of Jesus. Then Pilate ordered it to be given to him. And Joseph took the body and wrapped it in a clean linen shroud and laid it in his own new tomb, which he had cut in the rock. And he rolled a great stone to the entrance of the tomb and went away." (Matt. 27:57–60)

23. 1000 B.C.: David prophesies that Jesus would resurrect from death. 700 B.C.: Isaiah prophesies the same.

Promise: "For you will not abandon my soul to Sheol, or let your holy one see corruption." (Ps. 16:10); "Yet it was the will of the Lord to crush him; he has put him to grief; when his soul makes an offering for guilt, he shall see his offspring; he shall prolong his days; the will of the Lord shall proper in his hand. Out of the anguish of his soul he shall see and be satisfied; by his knowledge shall the righteous one, my servant, make many to be accounted righteous, and he shall bear their iniquities." (Isa. 53:10–11)

Fulfillment: "For David says concerning him, 'I saw the Lord always before me, for he is at my right hand that I may not be shaken; therefore my heart was glad, and my tongue rejoiced; my flesh also will dwell in hope. For you will not abandon my soul to Hades, or let your Holy One see corruption. You have made known to me the paths of life; you will make me full of gladness with your presence.' 'Brothers, I may say to you with confidence about the patriarch David that he both died and was buried, and his tomb is with us to this day. Being therefore a prophet, and knowing that God had sworn with an oath to him that he would set one of his descendants on his throne, he foresaw and spoke about the resurrection of the Christ, that he was not abandoned to Hades, nor did his flesh see corruption. This Jesus God raised up, and of that we all are witnesses...'" (Acts 2:25–32)

24. 1000 B.C.: David prophesies that Jesus would ascend into Heaven and take the souls of departed Christians with Him.

Promise: "You ascended on high, leading a host of captives in your train..." (Ps. 68:18)

Fulfillment: "But grace was given to each one of us according to the measure of Christ's gift. Therefore it says, 'When he ascended on high he led a host of captives, and he gave gifts to men.' ...He who descended is the one who also ascended far above all the heavens, that he might fill all things." (Eph. 4:7–10)

25. 1000 B.C.: David prophesies that Jesus would sit at the right hand of God.

Promise: "The Lord says to my Lord: 'Sit at my right hand, until I make your enemies your footstool.'" (Ps. 110:1)

Fulfillment: "He is the radiance of the glory of God and the exact imprint of his nature, and he upholds the universe by the word of his power. After making purification for sins, he sat down at the right hand of the Majesty on high..." (Heb. 1:3)

In summary, God's people knew their Savior Messiah Jesus Christ was coming because they carefully and prayerfully read the Old Testament Scriptures. Because those Scriptures were divinely inspired, they revealed future events surrounding the life, death, burial, Resurrection, and ascension of Jesus Christ in amazing detail. God alone is both knowledgeable of and sovereign over the details of future events, which explains biblical prophecy.

The presence of clear prophetic promises is one of the unique characteristics of Christianity and distinguishes it from every other world religion and cult. Regarding prophecy in the Bible,

> It is the only volume ever produced...in which is to be found a large body of prophecies relating to...the coming of One who was to be the Messiah. The ancient world had many different devices for determining the future, known as divination, but not in the entire gamut of Greek and Latin literature, even though they use the words prophet and prophecy, can we find any real specific prophecy of a great historic event to come in the distant future, nor any prophecy of a Savior to arise in the human race...[Islam] cannot point to any prophecies of the coming of Mohammed uttered hundreds of years before his birth. Neither can the founder of any cult . . . rightly identify any ancient text specifically foretelling their appearance.[60]

Regarding the importance of prophetic biblical prophecy about Jesus, a Bible scholar says:

> Some people have given such intensive study to the subject of prophecy that they have completely missed seeing the Lord Jesus Christ in their study of the Word. The Scripture was given to us to reveal Him. He is its Theme. He is the Center about which all the Scripture revolves...The first great result of the study of prophecy is that the prophetic Scriptures prove to us the authority of the entire Word of God. The Bible is different from every other religious book. There is no other book upon which a religion has been founded which includes prophecy within it...There is

no greater test or proof of the inspiration, validity, authority, and trustworthiness of the Bible than the proof of fulfilled prophecy.[61]

It is shocking that some flatly deny there is even one Old Testament prophecy regarding Jesus. Deist American revolutionary Thomas Paine said, "I have examined all the passages in the New Testament quoted from the Old, and so-called prophecies concerning Jesus Christ, and I find no such thing as a prophecy of any such person, and I deny there are any."[62]

The Bible prophesied the coming of Christ. There is simply no way to explain the specificity and variety of fulfilled prophecy in Scripture apart from the miraculous hand of God at work in the writing of Scripture: "The Old Testament, written over a 1,000-year period, contains several hundred references to the coming Messiah."[63]

Renowned seventeenth-century philosopher Blaise Pascal, a Christian mathematician who laid the foundations for the theory of probability concluded,

> If a single man had written a book foretelling the time and manner of Jesus's [sic] coming and Jesus had come in conformity with these prophecies, this would carry infinite weight. But there is much more here. There is a succession of men over a period of 4,000 years, coming consistently and invariably one after the other, to foretell the same coming; there is an entire people proclaiming it, existing for 4,000 years to testify in a body to the certainty they feel about it, from which they cannot be deflected by whatever threats and persecutions they may suffer. This is of a quite different order of importance.[64]

The bottom line is that Jesus' fulfillment of specific Old Testament messianic prophecies is far beyond any coincidence. This fact is one of the strongest arguments that God the Holy Spirit wrote the Bible through human authors, as God alone rules and reveals the future, and that Jesus Christ is exactly who the Bible says He is!

CHAPTER 4
WHAT WAS KING JESUS' FAMILY LIKE?

...coming to [Jesus'] hometown he taught them in their synagogue, so that they were astonished, and said, "Where did this man get this wisdom and these mighty works? Is not this the carpenter's son? Is not his mother called Mary? And are not his brothers James and Joseph and Simon and Judas? And are not all his sisters with us? Where then did this man get all these things?" –Matthew 13:54-56

Every Christmas, the world celebrates the birth of Jesus to His young mother, Mary, and decorates their homes with nativity scenes. Amazingly, God came into human history and had a family that includes a mother, adoptive father, half-brothers and sisters, as well as aunts, uncles, and cousins that are all mentioned in the Bible. We will get to know Jesus' family better, starting with His mother, Mary.

MOTHER MARY

Jesus' mother Mary was likely a teenager and grew up in the small town of Nazareth with a poor family. She was betrothed to Joseph, who likely grew up with her. In that culture, betrothal was a bit like engagement, but far more binding. To cancel a betrothal actually required a divorce.

Looking forward to her wedding day, Mary's dreams of a simple life are shattered. Luke 1:26-38 says,

> ...the angel Gabriel was sent from God to a city of Galilee named Nazareth, to a virgin betrothed to a man whose name was Joseph, of the house of David. And the virgin's name was Mary. And he came to her and said, "Greetings, O favored one, the Lord is with you!" But she was greatly troubled at the saying, and tried to discern what sort of greeting this might be. And the angel said to her, "Do not be afraid, Mary, for you have found favor with God. And behold, you will conceive in your womb and bear a son, and you shall call his name Jesus. He will be great and will be called the Son of the Most High. And the Lord God will give to him the throne of his father David, and he will

reign over the house of Jacob forever, and of his kingdom there will be no end." And Mary said to the angel, "How will this be, since I am a virgin?" And the angel answered her, "The Holy Spirit will come upon you, and the power of the Most High will overshadow you; therefore the child to be born will be called holy—the Son of God. And behold, your relative Elizabeth in her old age has also conceived a son, and this is the sixth month with her who was called barren. For nothing will be impossible with God." And Mary said, "Behold, I am the servant of the Lord; let it be to me according to your word." And the angel departed from her.

Mary is an outstanding example of faith in Jesus. Imagine her emotions when she's told by an angel that she will be pregnant without being married in a society that shamed, humiliated, exiled, or even killed such women! Tradition says they could have taken her to the gate of the city, ripped off her clothes, dressed her in rags, tied her up, and brought all the women to see her and learn the lesson of shame through her suffering.

But Mary believed the promises of Isaiah 7:14. She lived by the power of God with full faith in God. Protestant Reformer Martin Luther said that God giving her a son and faith in His promise were two great miracles in Mary's life.[65]

The first snapshot of the early church singles out Mary for mention as a woman of prayer. She was among the 120 people in the Upper Room worshiping Jesus as the only God before the Holy Spirit was poured out on the day of Pentecost.[a]

Mary is a wonderful example for all Christians, particularly women, and especially young women. She loved God, and, while not sinless like her son, she did live in holiness, as marked by her virginity until marriage and until after Jesus was born in obedience to God. She is an inspiring example that our sexually promiscuous culture desperately needs to have modeled. We all need to follow her example of humble faith that fully trusted

---

[a] Acts 1:13-14

God's will for her life. What makes Mary most famous, of course, is the virgin birth of Jesus Christ.

WHAT SCRIPTURE DOES TEACH ABOUT THE VIRGIN BIRTH OF JESUS

The prophetic promises of Jesus' virgin birth begin right after sin enters the world. In Genesis 3:15, God tells the Serpent, "I will put enmity between you and the woman, and between your offspring and her offspring; he shall bruise your head, and you shall bruise his heel." God promises that Jesus would be born from a woman. This is unusual because the rest of Scripture speaks of children as being born from their father.[a] Here, however, no father is mentioned for Jesus, which implies that He would not have a biological earthly father. Paul speaks in the same manner, saying, "But when the fullness of time had come, God sent forth his Son, born of a woman . . ."[b]

Some 700 years before the birth of Jesus, the prophet Isaiah further illuminated His virgin birth, saying, "Therefore the Lord himself will give you a sign. Behold, the virgin shall conceive and bear a son, and shall call his name Immanuel."[c] This verse is the most hotly debated Old Testament verse regarding the virgin birth of Jesus on two fronts.

Some contend that the prophecy was not speaking of future events but rather the ancient birth of the son of Ahaz. That is half true. The entire context reveals that the prophecy has a dual fulfillment; it speaks of the birth of a son to "Ahaz," as well as the birth of the Messiah to the "house of David."[d] Furthermore, by naming the son "Immanuel," God is promising more than just a male baby. Immanuel means "God is with us," which points to the son being God. A few pages later, we read,

For to us a child is born, to us a son is given; and the government shall be upon his shoulder, and his name shall be called Wonderful Counselor, Mighty God, Everlasting Father, Prince of Peace. Of the increase of his

---

[a] For example, Genesis 5 and 11 [b] Gal 4:4 [c] Isa 7:14 [d] Isa 7:10-14

government and of peace there will be no end, on the throne of David and over his kingdom, to establish it and to uphold it with justice and with righteousness from this time forth and forevermore. The zeal of the Lord of hosts will do this.[a]

This promise speaks to much more than just the birth of a male human baby.

Some also contend that the prophecy in Isaiah does not refer to a virgin. They argue that the Hebrew word *almah* (which is used in Isaiah 7:14) typically means "young woman," not "virgin," whereas the Hebrew word *bethulah* typically means "virgin." There are many reasons why the verse should be read as referring to a virgin. Even if the word does mean "young woman," that does not mean that she would not be a virgin. In that day, young women were virgins, making the terms synonymous for most young Hebrew women. If there was any question about her virginity, a woman was subject to physical inspection.[b]

Additionally, the word *almah* is used elsewhere in the Old Testament in reference to a young virgin woman. Rebekah, who is described as "a maiden [*bethulah*] whom no man had known."[c] Furthermore, Rebekah was a "virgin [*almah*]."[d] While the two words are virtually synonymous, *bethulah* required a bit more clarification that the woman was a virgin, while *almah* did not. Furthermore, two centuries before Jesus was born, the Jews understood exactly what *almah* means: the Septuagint, the Jewish 250 B.C. translation of the Hebrew Bible into Greek, translates *almah* as *parthenos*, which unambiguously means "virgin." Lastly, in the New Testament, Isaiah 7:14 is clearly interpreted to be a prophetic promise about the birth of Jesus to Mary, who was both a young woman and a virgin.

The fulfillment of the inference in Genesis and the promise in Isaiah are recorded in great historical detail in two of the four Gospels, namely Matthew 1:18–25 and Luke 1:26–38. In summary, the Old Testament both quietly implies and loudly

---

[a] Isa 9:6-7 [b] Deuteronomy 22:14–22 [c] Gen 24:16 [d] Gen 24:43

prophesies the virgin birth of Jesus. The writers of the New Testament go to painstaking detail to emphasize that, in every way, Jesus' mother, Mary, was a virgin woman who conceived Jesus solely through a miracle of God the Holy Spirit. Sadly, a number of false teachings have surrounded the virgin birth, which we will correct next.

WHAT SCRIPTURE DOES NOT TEACH ABOUT THE VIRGIN BIRTH OF JESUS

1. Scripture Does Not Teach That Mary Remained a Virgin for the Rest of Her Life

Arguments for the perpetual virginity of Mary arose as early as the second century, became more popular in the fourth century, and culminated with the Second Council of Constantinople in A.D. 553 declaring Mary "ever virgin." Some early church fathers (e.g., Origen), Catholic and Protestant theologians (e.g., Martin Luther, John Calvin, Ulrich Zwingli, and John Wesley), along with the Second Helvetic Confession and the Geneva Bible, say that Mary was "ever virgin," or semper virgo.

The implications of the perpetual virginity of Mary are many. Practically, this would mean that, following Jesus' birth, Mary never had intimate relations with her own husband, Joseph. This teaching is inaccurate for three reasons. First, God designed marriage to include physical union[a], and depriving marital intimacy is a sin.[b] Second, Matthew 1:25 implies that they did have relations following Jesus' birth: "[he] knew her not until she had given birth to a son. And he called his name Jesus." "Until" carries the strong implication that they had normal marital relations after Jesus was born. Third, Scripture repeatedly states that Mary had other sons and daughters, proving she and Joseph had a healthy married sex life.[c]

---

[a] Gen 2:24 [b] Gen 2:24 [c] Matt 12:46-50; 13:55-57; Mark 3:31-35; 6:3-4; Luke 8:19-21; John 2:12; 7:3,5,10; Acts 1:14; 1 Cor 9:5; Gal 1:19

2. Scripture Does Not Teach that Jesus' Virgin Birth Was a Myth Taken from Other Religions

In mythology, there are stories such as Zeus begetting Hercules and Apollo begetting Ion and Pythagoras. As a result, some have speculated that Christians stole the virgin birth story from such myths.

Ancient religions often taught bizarre supernatural origins but not virgin births. The Greeks said Hercules came from the sexual union of the god Zeus and the woman Alcmene. But that is hardly a virgin birth. Some sects of Hinduism believe Krishna is the virgin-born avatar or incarnation of Vishnu. But they also think Vishnu came as a fish, a turtle, a boar, a lion, and other bizarre things. Augustus Caesar also claimed a god impregnated his mother, Olympia, using a snake.

This speculation must be rejected on three grounds. First, some such myths came after the prophesy of Isaiah 7:14 and therefore could not have been the origination of the story. Second, the myths speak of gods having sex with women, which is not what the virgin birth account entails. Third, the myths do not involve actual human beings like Mary and Jesus but rather fictional characters like our modern-day comic book superheroes. If you check the facts, it becomes obvious that the teaching of the virgin birth of Jesus is unique.

3. Scripture Does Not Teach That Our Sin Nature Passed Only Through the Male Line

Many Christian theologians, including Aurelius Augustine, Aurelius Ambrose, Thomas Aquinas, and Martin Luther, believe sin nature is imparted through the male line. If this is true, then logically Jesus had to be virgin-born. Otherwise, an earthly father would have given Jesus a sin nature and brought Him under Adamic condemnation.

While Scripture clearly teaches that the sin of Adam brings death and condemnation to us all[a], it does not teach that our

---

[a] Rom. 5:12-21

sin nature comes only from our fathers. In fact, the Bible connects sinfulness with the normal process of conception, saying in Psalm 51:5, "Behold, I was brought forth in iniquity, and in sin did my mother conceive me." Furthermore, Scripture teaches that both genders are equally sinful, not that women are less sinful.[a]

Going even further, the Roman Catholic Church followed Augustine and said that Mary was not a sinner in her life. They teach that she, too, was immaculately conceived and therefore had no sin nature and was not a sinner. None of this is grounded in Scripture and flatly contradicts Mary's own words that she needed a savior.[b] Also, if she had no sin of any kind, why would she have brought a sin offering to the temple?[c] Indeed, Jesus was without sin[d] and did not have a sin nature, not because Mary was without sin, but because He was protected by a miracle of the Holy Spirit in a way that was similar to the miracles of God, making Adam from dust, granting Sarah the ability to conceive Isaac. While this point may seem trivial, if science such as genetic engineering continues to advance, we will probably see a cloned woman, and we don't believe that woman will be sinless!

4. Scripture Does Not Teach That Mary Slept with God

The Mormon cult teaches that God the Father once existed as a man, with a physical body. In his sermon the King Follet Discourse, Joseph Smith, the founder of Mormonism, said, "God himself was once as we are now, and is an exalted man, and sits enthroned in yonder heavens!" He went on to say that God "was once a man like us; yea, that God himself, the Father of us all, dwelt on an earth."[66]

5. Scripture Does Not Teach that Jesus' Virgin Birth is Unimportant

The only alternative to the virgin birth offered in Scripture

---

[a] Rom. 3:23 [b] Luke 1:46-47 [c] Luke 2:22-24 cf. Lev 12:6-8 [d] 2 Cor 5:21; Heb 4:15

is that Mary was a sexually sinful woman who conceived Jesus illegitimately, which was the accusation in Jesus' day.[a] In agreement, "theologian" and Jesus Seminar fellow Robert Funk has called Jesus a "bastard messiah."[67]

If the virgin birth of Jesus is untrue, then the story of Jesus changes dramatically; we would have a sexually promiscuous young woman lying about God's miraculous hand in the birth of her son, raising that son to declare he is God, and then joining His religion.[b] If Mary is nothing more than a sinful con artist, then neither she nor her son Jesus should be trusted.

The Bible is emphatic that Jesus' mother, Mary, was a virgin who conceived by the Holy Spirit. If we deny the virgin birth, we are flatly and plainly stating that Scripture may contain mistakes or even outright lies. In his book *The Virgin Birth of Christ*, which is perhaps the greatest book written defending this fact, Bible scholar J. Gresham Machen said, "Everyone admits that the Bible represents Jesus as having been conceived by the Holy Ghost and born of the Virgin Mary. The only question is whether in making that representation the Bible is true or false."[68] Machen went on to argue that "if the Bible is regarded as being wrong in what it says about the birth of Christ, then obviously the authority of the Bible in any high sense, is gone."[69]

A religious scholar also says, "Everything that we know of the dogmatics of the early part of the second century agrees with the belief that at that period the virginity of Mary was a part of the formulated Christian belief."[70]

FATHER JOSEPH

In accepting God's calling to be Jesus' earthly parents, culturally we may not completely appreciate what Mary and Joseph were willing to sacrifice. Mary risked losing her fiancé and her reputation. Joseph probably realized his boy Jesus would be called illegitimate, his wife would be called unfaithful, and he would be called a fool for the rest of his life.

---

[a] Matt 13:55; Mark 6:3; John 8:41 [b] Acts 1:14

His reputation would be ruined for marrying a sinful woman, bringing her shame into his life. He didn't have to accept this fate and could cancel the wedding. He is seemingly a strong and steady kind of guy who does a lot more than he says. When Gabriel visits him and tells him what's going on, he obeys the Lord, no matter the cost.

Since Jesus will not be his biological son, Joseph stands as a hero for foster parents, adoption, and blended families. He appears to be a quiet, humble, godly man, whose most significant ministry will turn out to be working an honest job, loving his wife, obeying God, and raising godly kids who change the world. Thanks to Joseph's humble obedience, Jesus had a devoted dad.

When we think of Jesus, we tend to remember Him as a grown man. However, it is helpful, especially as we train children, to remember that Jesus was also a child who matured for four reasons.

1. Jesus matured because He knew the Scriptures.

Luke 2:46–47 says that, at the age of 12 in the temple in Jerusalem, Jesus was "sitting among the teachers, listening to them and asking them questions." Jesus' knowledge of the Scriptures was so insightful that "all who heard him were amazed at his understanding and his answers."

2. Jesus lived in relationship with God the Father.

When Jesus' parents asked why He had been in the temple discussing the Bible for days, Jesus said in Luke 2:49, "I must be in my Father's house..." In the Old Testament, there are roughly only 15 references to God as Father. None of these speak of God being father of individuals but instead as father of the nation of Israel.

However, everything changed regarding our understanding of God as Father with the coming of Jesus Christ. Jesus' favorite name for God was *Father*, a term of endearment often referred to in the original language Jesus spoke as *Abba*. It appears roughly 165 times in the four Gospels.

One reason Jesus matured was His constant, warm, loving, and intimate relationship with God the Father as the beloved Son. Jesus encouraged us to have this same kind of relationship with the Father, teaching us to pray in Matthew 6:9, "Our Father..."

Building on the theme of maturing through a personal relationship with God the Father, Romans 8:14–16 says, "For all who are led by the Spirit of God are sons of God. For you did not receive the spirit of slavery to fall back into fear, but you have received the Spirit of adoption as sons, by whom we cry, 'Abba! Father!' The Spirit himself bears witness with our spirit that we are children of God." By being Spirit-empowered like Jesus, people can know God as Father and mature as Jesus did.

3. Jesus matured because He had respect for parental authority.

Luke 2:51–52 (NIV) summarizes Jesus' years from age 12 onward, saying, "...he went down to Nazareth with [His parents, Joseph and Mary] and was obedient to them...And Jesus grew in wisdom and stature, and in favor with God and man."

Though perfect, Jesus submitted to imperfect parents and honored His mother and father as the Ten Commandments required. If there was ever anyone who had the right to refuse to submit to any human authority, it was Jesus Christ. Jesus Christ matured, in part, because He honored and submitted to the parental authority that God placed over Him. The same is true of our maturing. Those who do not submit to authority do not mature. God works through authority and blesses those who honor authority.

4. Jesus matured by the power of the Holy Spirit.

Jesus' name Christ literally means the one anointed with the person, presence, and power of the Holy Spirit. A Bible dictionary says,

> Israel anticipated the arrival of the Anointed One, who would not be anointed by men and with oil prepared by human hands, but by God, with the Holy Spirit (Matt. 3:16–17 par. Mark 1:10–11; Luke 3:21–22). For that reason Jesus could testify of himself: "The Spirit of the Lord God is upon me, because the Lord has anointed me …" (Luke 4:18 quoting Isa. 61:1; cf. Acts 10:38). Thus, the name "Christ" connotes not only his sacred commission as Mediator and Redeemer of his people, but also the authority and power through which he was able to complete this mission.[71]

Luke 2:40 says of Jesus, "And the child grew and became strong, filled with wisdom. And the favor of God was upon him." Regarding His age, most Bible commentators agree that this refers to Jesus as a younger child under the age of 12 years old. Luke 2:52 then says, "Jesus increased in wisdom and in stature and in favor with God and man." Jesus had a family, obeyed His parents, and sets the perfect example of how a child matures in their relationship with God.

JESUS' EXTENDED FAMILY

Jesus' family had a godly legacy. Luke 1:5–7 says,

> …there was a priest named Zechariah…And he had a wife from the daughters of Aaron, and her name was Elizabeth. And they were both righteous before God, walking blamelessly in all the commandments and statutes of the Lord. But they had no child, because Elizabeth was barren, and both were advanced in years.

Elizabeth comes from generations of ministers, and Zechariah is a priest—the equivalent in those days of a rural pastor in a small town—also born into a ministry family. Zechariah and Elizabeth love the Lord, serve faithfully in

ministry, and wait until old age for God to bless them with
a child, which happened with the birth of their son John the
Baptizer. The angel Gabriel tells them their miracle baby will be
named John (meaning God is gracious): "And he will turn many
of the children of Israel to the Lord their God, and he will go
before him in the spirit and the power of Elijah…to make ready
for the Lord a people prepared" (vv. 16–17).

Jesus' relatives do not have fame, money, or power, but
they both have the Holy Spirit. Luke 1:41 says that "Elizabeth
was filled with the Holy Spirit" and then prophesied over Mary.
In Luke 1:67, "Zechariah was filled with the Holy Spirit and
prophesied" over his son at birth. Not only are Jesus' relatives
Spirit-filled, but so is His mother.

Excited to see her relative Elizabeth and celebrate their
pregnancies, Mary walks many miles to share their joy. In Luke
1:39–40, it says, "In those days Mary arose and went with haste
into the hill country, to a town in Judah, and she entered the
house of Zechariah and greeted Elizabeth."

The two pregnant women draw near one another, and with
them the two sons who represent the old covenant and the new
covenant, the promises and the fulfillment, the prophet and the
Lord. Their bellies come together—and Elizabeth's unborn son
John worships Jesus along with his mother! Luke 1:41 reports
that "the baby leaped in her womb. And Elizabeth was filled
with the Holy Spirit…"

This is incredible.

John is known by God, filled with the Spirit, and named
with a calling of destiny on his life from the womb. He is filled
with the Holy Spirit, and we get our first glimpse of John as an
in-utero worship leader, dancing and celebrating in the womb.
I can't think of a stronger portrait of personhood in the womb
than that.

Luke, a medical doctor, writes this report under the
inspiration of God the Holy Spirit. What does it mean when
he says of Elizabeth that "the baby leaped in her womb"? What
does the Bible mean by the word "baby"? An examination
of every time Luke uses the Greek word *brephos* shows a
consistency.

- Luke 1:41 – "…when Elizabeth heard the greeting of Mary, the baby leaped in her womb."
- Luke 1:44 – "…the baby [John the Baptizer] in my womb leaped for joy."
- Luke 2:12 – "…you will find a baby [Jesus] wrapped in swaddling cloths and lying in a manger."
- Luke 2:16 – "…they…found Mary and Joseph, and the baby lying in a manger."
- Luke 18:15-16 – "…they were bringing even infants to [Jesus] that he might touch them…Jesus called them to him, saying, 'Let the children come to me…'"
- Acts 7:19 – "[The godless Pharaoh] dealt shrewdly with our race and forced our fathers to expose their infants, so that they would not be kept alive."

The same word, *brephos*, is used for an unborn baby, a newborn baby, and a young child because God sees them all the same—as people bearing His image and likeness, worthy of all rights and dignity. A baby in a womb is known by God as John was, named by God as John was, and can be filled with God the Holy Spirit as John was.[a] How wonderful is it that God cares about unborn children? How encouraging is it that even when children are miscarried or aborted, we see the possibility that God can know them, love them, name them, and fill them with the Spirit even from the womb as He did John?

In John's public ministry, he preaches a lot of sermons, baptizes perhaps thousands of people, hands his ministry to Jesus, and gets martyred—all by the age of about 30.

Many, if not most, of Jesus' early followers are originally part of John's ministry. John accepts his role as the opening band and exits the stage once the crowd is warmed up, and Jesus is ready to take the stage. The Holy Spirit helps John to have a humble spirit, and Jesus calls him the greatest man who has ever lived.[b] The same is true of Jesus' brothers.

---

[a] Luke 1:15 [b] Matthew 11:11

JESUS' BROTHERS WERE SPIRIT-FILLED

Beyond a few of their names, we know very little about Jesus' brothers and sisters except for His half-brothers, James and Jude.

Jesus' half-brother[a], James is not a believer until Jesus appears to him following the Resurrection[b]. He is with the apostles at Pentecost[c] and becomes a leader of the Jerusalem church[d]. His nicknames are "James the Just" for his character and "Camel Knees" from praying so much.

In Jude 1, the author introduces himself as, "Jude, a servant of Jesus Christ and brother of James." In Galatians 2:9, Paul calls James a pillar holding up the Church along with Cephas (Peter) and John. Both James and Jude go on to be devoted Christian pastors, worshiping their big brother Jesus and writing books of the Bible bearing their names. James also presides over the conference held in Jerusalem to welcome Gentile converts in the church.[e]

According to tradition, James dies a martyr's death in service to his half-brother. We read that "James the half-brother of Jesus was executed…he was thrown off the temple and, still alive, was stoned to death."[72]

Dying, James echoes his big brother Jesus from Luke 23:34, saying, "Forgive them, for they know not what they do." One archaeological expert says, "When James is murdered…it is Simon…who takes over leadership of the movement."[73]

History seems to indicate that, to replace James, another one of Jesus' brothers named Simon (sometimes called Simeon) is chosen to assume leadership. If accurate, Mary and Joseph have at least three children in significant ministry roles in addition to their son Jesus Christ. Two of their sons wrote books of the Bible, and every book of the Bible is about their Son and Savior, Jesus Christ. Most of us are familiar with Jesus' ministry and its impact on history, but we often overlook the enormous role Jesus' family played in His ministry. Jesus had no ministry without His family!

---

[a] Matt. 13:55 [b] Mark 3:21; 1 Cor. 15:7 [c] Acts 1:14 [d] Gal. 1:19, 2:9; Acts 12:17, 15:12–21 [e] Acts 15

CHAPTER 5

WHAT WAS KING JESUS' RELATIONSHIP WITH SATAN, DEMONS, ANGELS, GOD THE FATHER, AND THE HOLY SPIRIT?

And Jesus, full of the Holy Spirit, returned from the Jordan and was led by the Spirit in the wilderness for forty days, being tempted by the devil. – Luke 4:1-2

When most people think about Jesus Christ's time on the earth, they reflect on His interaction and relationship with human beings – interacting with His disciples, surrounded by children, arguing with religious critics, and healing the sick as well as teaching. However, the Bible is clear that Jesus also had interactions and relationships with divine beings. These would include demons and angels, along with God the Father and God the Holy Spirit, and with Satan himself. We will study each of these relationships Jesus had with divine beings, starting with Satan.

A *Newsweek* article headline says, "Satan is Getting Hot as Hell in American Pop Culture." It reports, "Pew Research reported that 62 percent of American adults believe in Hell, up from 58 percent in 2014, and pop culture appears to be taking full advantage of the curiosity that surrounds Hell and its inhabitants."[74]

The article goes on to describe the explosion of interest in the satanic and supernatural in everything from movies to podcasts. The interest in demonic possession, exorcisms, and the paranormal work of demons masquerading as ghosts is incredibly popular. This interest should pull people into the Bible to learn about Jesus' relationship with Satan.

JESUS' RELATIONSHIP WITH SATAN

In many ways, the Bible serves as a battlefield report of a war that has been raging throughout human history. According to the Bible, angels are spirit beings created by God to serve His purposes. However, one angel became proud and preferred to be his own god rather than worship and obey the real God.[a] We now know him as Satan, the dragon, the serpent, the Enemy, the devil, the tempter, the murderer, the father of lies, the

---

[a] Isa. 14:11–23; Ezek. 28:12

adversary, the accuser, the destroyer, and the evil one.

Tragically, one-third of the angels sided with Satan to declare war on God and become the army devoted to destroying God's Kingdom[a]. Their rebellion culminated in a great battle against God and His holy angels.

After the great war in Heaven, continuing with the story of Scripture, the scene shifts to a new battlefield—earth. The Bible opens with a wedding between Adam and Eve, and by the time you turn the page, Satan the serpent shows up to declare war on their marriage and family.

Regretfully, our first parents surrendered to Satan and sinned and, ever since, everyone has suffered. Every one of us born since the fatal, foolish Fall has entered a spiritual war between the Kingdom of God and spiritual terrorists seeking only to kill, steal, and destroy.

God made a promise after our first parents, Adam and Eve, surrendered to sin. God Himself foretold the coming of Jesus to crush Satan, saying in Genesis 3:15, "I will put enmity between you and the woman, and between your offspring and her offspring; he shall bruise your head, and you shall bruise his heel." The battle was brewing.

Many years later, Jesus was born. The temptation of Jesus by Satan is so important that three Gospels (Matthew, Mark, and Luke) include it.

Jesus (also called "the last Adam" in 1 Corinthians 15:45) picks up the war where the first Adam fell in battle. Adam began with no sin nature, lived in a paradise, enjoyed a close friendship with God, endured temptation, failed, and was cast into the lonely wilderness. Jesus came with no sin nature, left a paradise, enjoyed a close friendship with God, endured temptation, succeeded, and defeated the dragon in the lonely wilderness.

Luke 4:1-15 records Jesus being tempted by Satan after fasting in solitude for 40 days. At the limits of His humanity, Jesus overcame demonic temptation by living in the continual presence of God, the Holy Spirit. Jesus' temptation account

---

[a] Isa. 14:12; Luke 10:18; Heb. 12:22; Rev. 9:1, 12:3–9

begins in Luke 4:1, which says, "Jesus, full of the Holy Spirit..." The temptation account ends in verses 14–15, where Luke says, "Jesus returned in the power of the Spirit..." Jesus' spiritual victory begins and ends with being Spirit-filled. This is the key to spiritual warfare and defeating demonic temptation. Jesus said in Matthew 12:28, "...if it is by the Spirit of God that I cast out demons, then the kingdom of God has come upon you." Jesus clearly stated that He defeated demons by the power of the Holy Spirit—the same power we have access to as Christians.

SATAN'S ATTACKS ON JESUS

Satan's attack on Jesus also commenced when Jesus was only a boy. In an attempt to murder Jesus as an infant, King Herod decreed the execution of all firstborn sons. Through an angel, God warned Jesus' parents of the plot, and they fled to Egypt as refugees to spare Jesus' life.

The backdrop of the entire life of Jesus is spiritual warfare. Leading up to the cross, Satan nearly got Peter to join the demonic rebellion, but Jesus prayed for him: "Simon, Simon, behold, Satan demanded to have you, that he might sift you like wheat, but I have prayed for you..."[a] Satan will try and recruit you into his rebellion as well, but the good news is that Jesus continually prays for you as He "always lives to make intercession..."[b]

Judas Iscariot connected with Satan[c] and conspired with him to betray Jesus and hand Him over to be crucified. All of this was spiritual warfare. Through the cross, Satan and his demons thought they had finally defeated Jesus. Isaiah 45:15 says, "Truly, you are a God who hides himself, O God of Israel, the Savior." On the cross Jesus hid His victory in defeat, hid His glory in shame, and hid our life in His death.

On the cross Jesus bled and died for you. Jesus' words, "It is finished," from the cross are His heralding of your deliverance. Crucifying Jesus was the biggest mistake the devil

---

[a] Luke 22:31-32 [b] Heb. 7:25 [c] Heb. 7:25

ever made. "None of the rulers of this age understood this, for if they had, they would not have crucified the Lord of glory."[a] Satan and the demons did not see their fatal mistake because they lacked the sight of faith and did not understand the humility of Jesus.

JESUS THE DRAGON SLAYER

One of the most emotionally powerful Scriptures about Jesus' victory over Satan, sin, and death, says:

And you, who were dead in your trespasses and the uncircumcision of your flesh, God made alive together with him, having forgiven us all our trespasses, by canceling the record of debt that stood against us with its legal demands. This he set aside, nailing it to the cross. He disarmed the rulers and authorities and put them to open shame, by triumphing over them in him.[b]

The imagery in this verse from Colossians comes from the great battle victories celebrated in antiquity. Jesus is our dragon slayer who came to defeat our Enemy, the dragon, and set us free.

We long for the final defeat of the dragon with the return of Jesus. But the authority of the devil and his demons in our lives has already ended. Jesus has thoroughly freed us from all our obligations to and agreements with the dragon, enabling us to live according to the following scripture:

...walk in a manner worthy of the Lord, fully pleasing to him: bearing fruit in every good work and increasing in the knowledge of God...strengthened with all power, according to his glorious might, for all endurance and patience with joy; giving thanks to the Father, who has qualified you to share in the inheritance of the saints in light. He has delivered us from the domain of darkness and

----

[a] 1 Cor. 2:8 [b] Col. 2:13-15

transferred us to the kingdom of his beloved Son, in whom we have redemption, the forgiveness of sins.[a]

Though Jesus won the decisive victory in His death, Resurrection, and exaltation, Satan and his demons will not be destroyed until the final judgment at Jesus' white throne.[b] Subsequently, their work continues on the earth, which means you must walk wisely. The devil and his demons have no legal authority over any believer. They may take advantage of our sin, folly, weakness, fear, or unbelief. However, their ownership, dominion, and condemnation of us were canceled at the cross of Christ. For those who belong to and believe in Christ, all demonic ties formed through sin, cultic vows, generational sin, and participation in the demonic realm were rendered null and void forever by virtue of the complete and total victory of Jesus Christ. Your ministry is to believe and exercise that authority.

JESUS' RELATIONSHIP WITH DEMONS

One of the more curious aspects of Jesus' earthly ministry is that people were often unable and/or unwilling to see Him as God. Jesus used the word "dull" to refer to such people who were as discerning as the guys who drive for miles with their turn signal on.[c] The exception to this rule, shockingly enough, was the demons. While many people said Jesus was demon-possessed and raving mad, the demons were more likely to get it right.

The Gospel of Mark gets right to the point. Jesus stirs up a ruckus when He comes to town. He calls, and tough men follow Him. He teaches, and people are astonished. But it's the demons who know in Mark 1:24: "What have you to do with us, Jesus of Nazareth? Have you come to destroy us? I know who you are—the Holy One of God."

Mark 1:33–34 says, "the whole city was gathered together at the door. And he healed many who were sick with various diseases, and cast out many demons. And he would not permit

---
[a] Col. 1:10-14 [b] Rev. 20:11-15 [c] Matthew 13:15

the demons to speak, because they knew him." Luke 4:33–34 says,

> And in the synagogue there was a man who had the spirit of an unclean demon, and he cried out with a loud voice, "Ha! What have you to do with us, Jesus of Nazareth? Have you come to destroy us? I know who you are—the Holy One of God."

In Luke 4:40–41, we read,

> Now when the sun was setting, all those who had any who were sick with various diseases brought them to him, and he laid his hands on every one of them and healed them. And demons also came out of many, crying, "You are the Son of God!" But he rebuked them and would not allow them to speak, because they knew that he was the Christ.

Demons appear to have some of the highest views of Jesus in the Gospels, but they do not love Him or receive salvation. The demons even have a higher view of Jesus than most present-day cults and world religions as well as progressive, apostate pastors.

Throughout the Gospels, while people, including Jesus' own disciples, are uncertain if He is God at times, the one group that continually recognizes Him as God is the demons. The problem with demons is not that they are unaware of who Jesus is but that they are unwilling to worship Jesus as God. They are determined to wage war against Him out of loyalty to their false god, the fallen angel known as Satan.

Jesus demonstrated His divine authority over demons with deliverance ministry. The Bible records four occasions where Jesus delivered someone from the demonic:

1. Deliverance in a synagogue[a]
2. Deliverance for the demoniac man[b]

---

[a] Mark 1:21-28; Luke 4:31-37 [b] Matthew 8:28-34; Mark 5:1-20; Luke 8:26-40

3. Deliverance for a Syrophoenician girl[a]
4. Deliverance for a young boy[b]

These divine deliverances reveal Jesus healing men and women, adults and children, and doing so both indoors at religious meeting places and outdoors in the wilderness. In short, Jesus can and does deliver anyone from the demonic anywhere because He has complete and total authority over every unclean demonic spirit.

JESUS' RELATIONSHIP WITH ANGELS

God sent an angel to tell Mary and Joseph that Jesus was coming. Can you imagine the enormity of this experience? No one ever went to the backwater town of Nazareth. Then, an angel appeared to announce the selection of an unlikely young woman for the most significant task ever given to a mere mortal.

This was just the beginning of angelic ministry in the life of Jesus. Angels served in Jesus' earthly life in 13 ways:

1. An angel promised the birth and ministry of John the Baptizer.[c]
2. An angel named Jesus.[d]
3. An angel told Mary she was chosen to be Jesus' virgin mother.[e]
4. An angel told Mary and Joseph to parent Jesus.[f]
5. Angels told the shepherds Jesus was born.[g]
6. Angels worshiped Jesus at His birth.[h]
7. Angels warned Jesus' parents of the coming genocide so they could flee to Egypt.[i]
8. Angels strengthened Jesus after His temptation battle with Satan.[j]
9. An angel strengthened Jesus in Gethsemane before the cross.[k]

---

[a] Matthew 15:21-28; Mark 7:24-30 [b] Matthew 17:14-21; Mark 9:14-29; Luke 9:37-43 [c] Luke 1:11-17 [d] Matt 1:21; Luke 1:13 [e] Matt 1:20-21; Luke 1:26-37 [f] Matt. 1:20-21 [g] Luke 2:8-15 [h] Luke 2:13-14 [i] Matt. 2:13,20 [j] Matt. 4:11 [k] Luke 22:43

10. An angel rolled the stone away from Jesus' tomb.[a]
11. An angel told two women at the empty tomb that Jesus had risen.[b]
12. Two angels comforted Mary Magdalene and reunited her with Jesus.[c]
13. Angels promised that Jesus would be coming again.[d] And still yet to come, angels will declare Jesus' victory and ride into history with Him for war in the end.[e]

JESUS' RELATIONSHIP WITH GOD THE FATHER

Prayer is mainly about relationship. Prayer does include needs being met, burdens being lifted, questions being answered, hurts being healed, joys being shared, and fears being conquered – but all those things are in the context of a loving parent-child relationship between God the Father and you.

The Old Testament talks a lot about fathers and includes genealogies listing generations of dads. God is referred to as Father only roughly 15 times, and those few occasions are in reference to God's relationship with the nation of Israel, not warm and personal communication to an individual. Everything changes with the coming of Jesus Christ. Jesus' favorite title for God is "Father."

A theological dictionary says,

The teaching of the Fatherhood of God takes a decided turn with Jesus, for "Father" was his favorite term for addressing God. It appears on his lips some sixty-five times in the Synoptic Gospels and over one hundred times in John. The exact term Jesus used is still found three times in the New Testament (Mark 14:36; Rom. 8:15–16; Gal. 4:6) but elsewhere the Aramaic term Abba is translated by the Greek patēr. The uniqueness of Jesus' teaching on this subject is evident for several reasons. For one, the rarity of this designation for God is striking. There is no evidence in pre-Christian Jewish literature that Jews

---

[a] Matt. 28:2 [b] Matt. 28:5-7; Luke 24:4-7; John 20:11-14 [c] John 20:11-14 [d] Acts 1:10-11 [e] Rev. 1:1; 19:9; 22:1, 6, 16

addressed God as "Abba." A second unique feature about Jesus' use of Abba as a designation for God involves the intimacy of the term. Abba was a term little children used when they addressed their fathers. At one time it was thought that since children used this term to address their fathers the nearest equivalent would be the English term "Daddy." More recently, however, it has been pointed out that Abba was a term not only that small children used to address their fathers; it was also a term that older children and adults used. As a result it is best to understand Abba as the equivalent of "Father" rather than "Daddy."[75]

When Jesus prayed to God as Father, He did so with warmth and reverence. In Mark 14:36, Jesus prays, "Abba, Father, all things are possible for you...Yet not what I will, but what you will." Heading to the cross, Jesus prayed in Luke 22:42, "Father, if you are willing, remove this cup from me. Nevertheless, not my will, but yours, be done." Throughout His life, Jesus' favorite title for God was Father, and He lived as an obedient Son.

Jesus taught us to pray to God as Father, like He did. The world's most famous prayer is found in Matthew 6, as Jesus taught His disciples how to pray, saying, "Pray then like this: Our Father..."

Jesus' relationship with God the Father was so perfect and pure that, according to the Bible, when we look at Jesus, we see God the Father reflected. Jesus said in John 14:7-8, "If you had known me, you would have known my Father also." Jesus was then asked, "show us the Father." We cannot see the Father like a human being in a body because He is invisible, immaterial, and spiritual. This also explains why the Ten Commandments forbid seeking to depict God the Father with any physical reality or graven image. However, this does not imply that the Father is not visible. Jesus Christ took upon Himself human flesh to enter human history and, in response to the question about seeing God the Father, Jesus says, "Whoever has seen me has seen the Father."

In the middle of this same discussion about getting to God the Father, Jesus summarized His entire earthly mission, saying in John 14:6, "I am the way, and the truth, and the life. No one comes to the Father except through me."

Importantly, the language of God the Father and God the Son is relational and not biological, as God the Father does not inhabit a physical body as Jesus did. Their one-of-a kind relationship is spoken of in English Bibles with the phrase "only begotten" or "only son."[a] A Bible encyclopedia explains, "The word traditionally translated 'only-begotten' does not carry the idea of birth at all. Literally it means 'only one of its kind,' 'unique.'" We are inclined to think this refers to what the Holy Spirit did in begetting Jesus in the womb of Mary.[76]

JESUS' RELATIONSHIP WITH THE HOLY SPIRIT

When someone is successful, their life is studied to find the secret to their success. Without peer, the life of Jesus Christ has left the greatest footprint in world history. The key to His success was His consistent reliance on the power of the Holy Spirit.

The ancient church creeds are very helpful, however there is one thing missing—how Jesus lived His life. Notice how each creed moves from the birth of Jesus to the death of Jesus and omits the entirety of His life. The Apostles' Creed (fourth century AD) says Jesus was "born of the Virgin Mary; suffered under Pontius Pilate, was crucified..." The Nicene Creed (fourth century AD) says Jesus "was incarnate by the Holy Ghost of the Virgin Mary, and was made man, and was crucified also for us under Pontius Pilate..."

What is missing? Jesus' earthly life. If we do not know how Jesus lived His life on earth, how are we supposed to know how to live our lives on earth?

Jesus lived in obscurity until His baptism. We know very little about His life during His teens and twenties, but all that changes at His baptism. The baptism of Jesus Christ is

-----
[a] e.g., John 1:14, 3:18; Luke 7:12, 8:42, 9:38; Hebrews 11:17

so significant that it appears in all four of the New Testament Gospels. Luke 3:21–22 reports,

> Now when all the people were baptized, and when Jesus also had been baptized and was praying, the heavens were opened, and the Holy Spirit descended on him in bodily form, like a dove; and a voice came from heaven, "You are my beloved Son; with you I am well pleased."

This event was not Jesus receiving the Holy Spirit for the first time. In the previous chapters, Luke clearly tells us that the Holy Spirit was intimately involved in the life and ministry of Jesus Christ from the womb. Mary, His mother, conceived Jesus by the power of the Holy Spirit. Therefore, at every moment of His journey into human history through the womb of Mary, the Spirit was present in power with Jesus. Jesus' baptism was not where He received the Spirit, but rather it was a public event where the Father "revealed" to the crowd what Jesus already knew—that He lived in loving and constant relationship with God the Father and God the Spirit.[a] Jesus' baptism was when He was anointed by and with the Holy Spirit for His ministry as the Messiah. This is akin to the anointing of kings and prophets in the Old Testament.[b] This was crucially important because God's people had long awaited the fulfillment of Isaiah's promises that their Savior would come in the power of the Spirit.

- Isaiah 11:2 – …the Spirit of the LORD shall rest upon him, the Spirit of wisdom and understanding, the Spirit of counsel and might, the Spirit of knowledge and the fear of the LORD.
- Isaiah 42:1 – My servant, whom I uphold, my chosen, in whom my soul delights; I have put my Spirit upon him…
- Isaiah 48:16 – …the Lord GOD has sent me, and his Spirit.
- Isaiah 61:1 – The Spirit of the Lord GOD is upon me,

---

[a] John 1:31 [b] 1 Sam. 16:13; 1 Kings 19:16

because the LORD has anointed me…

Since there is no authority higher than God the Father, His public validation was the highest validation possible to launch Jesus' public ministry following His baptism. The presence of the Spirit like a dove reminds us of the days of Noah. In that day, salvation from God's wrath came through deliverance via a wooden boat carrying God's people, and in Jesus' day, salvation from God's wrath would come via a wooden cross carried by God Himself.

Looking back at Jesus' baptism, Peter preaches in Acts 10:36–38:

> …preaching good news of peace through Jesus Christ (he is Lord of all), you yourselves know what happened throughout all Judea, beginning from Galilee after the baptism that John proclaimed: how God anointed Jesus of Nazareth with the Holy Spirit and with power. He went about doing good and healing all who were oppressed by the devil, for God was with him.

Peter says one of the primary purposes of Jesus' baptism was to publicly announce that Jesus' entire ministry—including preaching, healing, and delivering—would be accomplished by the power of the Holy Spirit. Matthew 3:16 reveals a curious detail that those present "saw the Spirit of God descending like a dove and coming to rest on him…" In John 1:32–33, John the Baptizer says, "I saw the Spirit descend from heaven like a dove, and it remained on him…he who sent me to baptize with water said to me, 'He on whom you see the Spirit descend and remain, this is he who baptizes with the Holy Spirit.'" The language of the Spirit "coming to rest" and "remain" on Jesus reveals an ongoing, abiding, and relational presence where everything in Jesus' life will be under the control and by the power of the Spirit.

Regarding the relationship between Jesus and the Holy Spirit, legendary Bible teacher Martin Lloyd-Jones says,

What, then, does all this mean? It means that there was no change in His deity, but that He took human nature to Himself, and chose to live in this world as a man. He humbled Himself in that way. He deliberately put limits upon Himself. Now we cannot go further. We do not know how He did it. We cannot understand it, in a sense. But we believe this: in order that He might live this life as a man, while He was here on earth, He did not exercise certain qualities of His Godhead. That was why…He needed to be given the gift of the Holy Spirit without measure.[77]

Theologian and former prime minister of the Netherlands Abraham Kuyper writes of the importance of the relationship between Jesus and the Holy Spirit:

This ought to be carefully noticed, especially since the Church has never sufficiently confessed the influence of the Holy Spirit exerted upon the work of Christ. The general impression is that the work of the Holy Spirit begins when the work of the Mediator on earth is finished, as tho [sic] until that time the Holy Spirit celebrated His divine day of rest. Yet the Scripture teaches us again and again that Christ performed His mediatorial work controlled and impelled by the Holy Spirit.[78]

In the book *Spirit-Filled Jesus*, I (Mark) write in detail about the personal relationship between Jesus Christ and the Holy Spirit and how we can live by His power as Jesus did. The empowerment of Jesus by God the Holy Spirit is repeatedly stressed in the Gospel of Luke, which precedes Acts in showing the Spirit-filled life of Christ and then Christians as the two-part history of our faith. Here is a summary:

1. Jesus was conceived by the Holy Spirit and given the title "Christ," which means anointed by the Holy

Spirit.[a]

2. Jesus' relative Elizabeth was "filled with the Holy Spirit" when greeting Jesus' pregnant mother Mary, and her husband Zechariah went on to prophesy in the Spirit that their son John was appointed by God to prepare the way for Jesus.[b]

3. An angel revealed to Mary that she would give birth to Jesus because "the Holy Spirit will come upon you."[c]

4. Once born, Jesus was dedicated to the Lord in the temple according to the demands of the law by Simeon; "the Holy Spirit was upon [Simeon]" and the Holy Spirit had revealed to him that he would not die until seeing Jesus Christ.[d]

5. Simeon was "in the Spirit" when he prophesied about Jesus' ministry to Jews and Gentiles.[e]

6. John prophesied in the Spirit that one day Jesus would baptize people with the Holy Spirit.[f]

7. The Holy Spirit descended upon Jesus at His own baptism.[g]

8. Jesus was "full of the Holy Spirit."[h]

9. Jesus was "led by the Spirit."[i]

10. Jesus came "in the power of the Spirit."[j]

11. After reading Isaiah 61:1–2, "The Spirit of the Lord GOD is upon me," Jesus declared, "Today this Scripture has been fulfilled in your hearing."[k]

12. Jesus "rejoiced in the Holy Spirit."[l]

A book written about Jesus' relationship with the Holy Spirit says, "[Jesus] is the supreme example for them of what is possible in a human life because of his total dependence upon the Spirit of God."[79]

How did Jesus Christ live His life and leave His legacy? By the Spirit. A Bible scholar says, "Jesus...is the supreme example...of what is possible in a human life because of his total dependence upon the Spirit of God.[80]

---

[a] Luke 1-2 [b] Luke 1:41-43, 67, 76 [c] Luke 1:35-37 [d] Luke 2:25-27 [e] Luke 2:27-34 [f] Matt. 3:11; Mar. 1:8; Luke 3:16; John 1:34 [g] Matt. 3:16; John 1:32-33 [h] Luke 4:1-2 [i] Luke 4:1-2 [j] Luke 4:14 [k] Luke 4:14-21 [l] Luke 10:21

It is common for Christians to speak about having a personal relationship with Jesus Christ. We absolutely encourage this.

Jesus, however, lived His life by a personal relationship with the Holy Spirit. Our Helper was also Jesus' Helper.

As God's person, the Holy Spirit is fully God and the third member of the Trinity.

As God's presence, the Holy Spirit is God with us.

As God's power, the Holy Spirit empowered the life of Jesus Christ and also empowers the life of believers to live by His power and become like Christ.

If Jesus were living your life, what would He be doing, and how would He be doing it? By the Spirit. That's the key that unlocks the rest of your life. We don't want you to live your life for Christ. We want Christ to live His life through you by the power of the Holy Spirit!

CHAPTER 6
HOW WERE JESUS' MIRACLES SIGNS OF HIS KINGDOM?

...Jesus answered them, "Go and tell...what you hear and see: the blind receive their sight and the lame walk, lepers are cleansed and the deaf hear, and the dead are raised up, and the poor have good news preached to them..." – Matthew 11:4-5

A worldview is like a set of glasses that shapes how you see everyone and everything. For the Christian, our worldview is established by the Bible. We do not merely look at the Bible; we also look through the Bible to understand everything in our life and world.

According to the Bible, there is one reality ruled by God over two realms: 1) the spirit world, where God, divine beings (including angels and demons), and departed people live right now, and 2) the physical world, where we as human beings live.

Originally, these two realms were connected. The Garden of Eden in Genesis was literally Heaven on earth, where the unseen and seen realms interlocked. This explains why Adam and Eve met with God there, were not shocked when a divine being showed up (Satan), and saw an angel keep them from the Tree of Life once they sinned. Miracles were constant until humanity sinned, and the realms were disconnected. So, upon death, the two parts of our being are also disconnected. Our body goes into the ground awaiting resurrection, while our spirit goes to be with God.

When Jesus returns to earth, He will bring Heaven with Him to restore things as they were before sin entered the world and establish the eternal Kingdom of God (also referred to as the Kingdom of Heaven in the Bible).

God does not change, and God does not change His plan for His people and His planet. This explains why the Bible uses lots of words like restore, redeem, resurrect, renew, etc., to speak about eternity. Acts 3:21 looks forward to "the time for restoring all..." God will go back to where He started to lift the curse, sentence Satan and demons to eternal torment, raise the dead, and make the realm of Eden in the unseen world visible in the seen realm of earth. He will overtake and liberate all that has been cursed by our sin to be cured by His Son. All of this divine work will be miraculous.

THIN PLACES

Until Jesus returns to bring the Kingdom once and forever, we have temporary Thin Places. Old Celtic Christians referred to the times when the unseen and seen realms intersected, and God showed up in supernatural, miraculous ways as Thin Places. When the two realms come together, miracles happen as the unseen realm invades and supersedes the seen realm.

In the Old Testament, things such as a divine ladder from Heaven to earth on which angels descended in the days of Jacob, a cloud by day and a pillar of fire by night in the days of Moses, a tabernacle, and a temple that housed God's presence closed the distance between the seen and unseen realms. Throughout the Old Testament, God's people have historically memorialized Thin Places by building altars and stacking stones of remembrance to mark these sacred spaces.

Thin Places prefigured the coming of Jesus Christ as the connecting point between God in Heaven and people on earth. 1 Timothy 2:5 says, "...there is one God, and there is one mediator between God and men, the man Christ Jesus..." In Jesus Christ, God became a man, and He became the Thin Place between Heaven and earth.

Miracles and other supernatural manifestations of divine power from the unseen realm appear in Thin Places. Subsequently, when God shows up in power, a common place becomes sacred, which explains why God told Moses in Exodus 3:5, "Do not come near; take your sandals off your feet, for the place on which you are standing is holy ground." Genesis 28:16-17 (NLT) says, "Then Jacob awoke from his sleep and said, 'Surely the LORD is in this place, and I wasn't even aware of it!' But he was also afraid and said, 'What an awesome place this is! It is none other than the house of God, the very gateway to heaven!'"

Miracles are the supernatural manifestations that happen when the seen and unseen realms come together. The Bible records around 127 miracles.[81] As you study Jesus' miracles in the Bible, remember that they fall into four categories:

1. Ruling over nature
2. Restoring health
3. Removing demons
4. Raising the dead[82]

Before we can know if a miracle has happened, we need to first define what a miracle is. Philosophers say that "a miracle (from the Latin *mirari*, to wonder) [is] an event that is not explicable by natural causes alone. A reported miracle excites wonder because it appears to require, as its cause, something beyond the reach of human action and natural causes."[83]

To keep things simple, we will use the following definition: A miracle is an event where a spiritual being supersedes the laws of nature. In this definition, there is the possibility that not only God but also angels and other divine beings (e.g., divine council, sons of God, the gods, the assembly of the holy ones, the council of the holy ones, hosts, the seat of the gods, the mount of assembly, the watchers, the court in judgment, and the Heavenly host) can do miracles. This definition also recognizes that fallen, sinful divine beings like Satan and demons can also perform counterfeit miracles. Simply put, a miracle is extraordinary, in contrast to the rest of life, which is ordinary.

WHY DO SOME PEOPLE NOT BELIEVE IN MIRACLES?

While the Bible is a record of miracles from beginning to end, many other worldviews do not believe that miracles are possible. Atheism comes from the negative *a-*, which means "no," "not," or "without," and *theos*, which means "god." Basically, atheism is the belief that there is no God. Related to atheism are the beliefs that there is no devil, demons, supernatural realm, miracles, or absolute moral truth over all cultures. According to them, nothing exists beyond the material world, leading them to believe that people do not have souls and that there is no possibility of spiritual life beyond physical death. Curiously, atheism is historically a relatively new concept. Atheist David Hume, most likely the greatest philosophical influence against the possibility of miracles, famously said, "A miracle is a violation of the laws of nature..."[84]

For Hume and other atheists, the world runs on inviolable natural laws that cannot be broken. As a result, our world is closed, and there is no one and no thing outside of the system who can break our natural laws and do miracles; therefore, miracles are impossible. This view of the world is called naturalism, the opposite of the biblical worldview, which is supernaturalism.

Deism teaches that a god made the universe but then left his creation alone and has no dealings with it, a bit like an absentee landlord. The world runs by natural laws that a god established to govern his creation. Subsequently, miracles are impossible because the universe is a closed system, and a god does not intervene in his creation or overrule his natural laws. Perhaps the most noted deist was President Thomas Jefferson (1743–1826). He sat down in the White House with a razor in one hand and the Bible in the other and cut out those parts of Scripture that he decided were untrue, mainly the miracles. The result was *The Philosophy of Jesus of Nazareth*, or *The Life and Morals of Jesus of Nazareth*. Only 990 Scripture verses survived, zero miracles were considered factual, and the Resurrection of Jesus was systematically cut from the pages of Scripture.

Those worldviews that flatly deny the possibility of a miracle are simply ignoring the reports of people throughout human history. Most cultures in world history have believed in miracles, and the small list of those who have not lived in more recent years with new prejudices and biases. For example, the rationalism behind atheism disbelieved most anything that could not be seen through a telescope or microscope and believed only that which could be proven through the scientific method of testing and re-testing. Since miracles are, by definition, non-repeatable, one-time events, they became impossible to believe. This led to naturalism, a worldview that all is material and nothing is spiritual.

The result was skepticism about the spiritual and, eventually, atheism and the denial of God altogether. In contrast, a scholar named Craig Keener wrote a comprehensive report of miracles in his more than 1100-page, two-volume series *Miracles: The Credibility of the New Testament Accounts.* He documents, in detail, verified miracles throughout human history in a variety of nations, cultures, and generations. Additionally, many of the New Testament miracles are reported in the books of Luke and Acts, both written by a medical doctor who gives medical confirmation of healings. Lastly, throughout the Bible, including in the days of Jesus, miracles were done in the presence of witnesses who testified—sometimes even in court under oath—to the genuineness of a supernatural miracle.

JESUS' MIRACLES

Here are Jesus' 33 miracles recorded in the Bible in chronological order[a]:

No.	Description	Matt.	Mark	Luke	John
1	Jesus turns water into wine				2:1–11
2	Jesus heals a nobleman's son				4:46–54
3	Jesus provides a large catch of fish			5:1–11	
4	Jesus delivers a man in a synagogue		1:21–28	4:31–37	
5	Jesus heals Peter's mother-in-law	8:14–17	1:29–31	4:38-39	
6	Jesus heals a leper	8:2–4	1:40–45	5:12–16	
7	Jesus heals a paralytic via roof	9:1–8	2:1–12	5:17–26	
8	Jesus heals a cripple by a pool				5:1–16

[a] This chronology is based on A. T. Robertson's *A Harmony of the Gospels.*

No.	Description	Matt.	Mark	Luke	John
9	Jesus heals a withered hand	12:9–14	3:1–6	6:6–11	
10	Jesus heals a centurion's servant	8:5–13		7:1–10	
11	Jesus raises a widow's son			7:11–17	
12	Jesus calms a storm	8:23–27	4:35–41	8:22–25	
13	Jesus delivers the demoniac man	8:28–34	5:1–20	8:26–40	
14	Jesus heals a bleeding woman	9:20–22	5:25–34	8:43–48	
15	Jesus raises Jairus' daughter	9:18–26	5:21–43	8:41–56	
16	Jesus heals two blind men	9:27–31			
17	Jesus feeds the 5,000	14:13–21	6:30–44	9:10–17	6:1–15
18	Jesus causes Peter to walk on water	14:22–33	6:45–52		6:15–21
19	Jesus delivers a Syrophoenician	15:21–28	7:24–30		
20	Jesus heals a deaf and mute man		7:31–37		
21	Jesus feeds the 4,000	15:32–39	8:1–9		
22	Jesus heals a blind man		8:22–26		

No.	Description	Matt.	Mark	Luke	John
23	Jesus delivers a young boy	17:14–21	9:14–21	9:37–43	
24	Jesus gets a coin from a fish	17:24–27			
25	Jesus heals a man born blind				9:1–38
26	Jesus heals a stooped woman			13:10–17	
27	Jesus heals a man with dropsy			14:1–6	
28	Jesus raises Lazarus				11:1–46
29	Jesus heals ten lepers			17:11–19	
30	Jesus heals blind Bartimaeus	20:29–34	10:46–52	18:35–43	
31	Jesus causes a fig tree to die	21:18–22	11:12–14		
32	Jesus heals Malchus' ear			22:49–51	
33	Jesus causes a big catch of fish				21:1–14

WHAT KINDS OF MIRACLES DID JESUS PERFORM?

There are two reasons it's surprising that we know so much about Jesus' miracles. One, Jesus often performed a miracle and then instructed the witnesses not to tell anyone. After Jesus healed a woman and a girl, Mark 5:43 says, "...he strictly charged them that no one should know this..." After healing a deaf man, Mark 7:36 says, "Jesus charged them to tell no one." After healing a blind man, Jesus told him in Mark 8:26 to avoid crowds who would see him healed, saying, "Do not even enter the village." Two, Jesus did far more miracles than those recorded in Scripture: "Now there are also many other things that Jesus did. Were every one of them to be written, I suppose that the world itself could not contain the books that would be written."[a]

Even Jesus' enemies recognized His miracles. Without denying His power, they weaponized the supernatural aspects of His ministry to attack Him for violating their religious rules, as "Seven of the 33 miracles of Christ were done on the Sabbath day."[85]

The miracle-working power of Jesus Christ is well-established not only in the Scriptures but outside of them as well. The Jewish Talmud charged that Jesus "practiced magic."[86] Celsus, a strong opponent of Christianity, later repeated that claim.[87] The noted Jewish historian Josephus also reported that Jesus was "a doer of wonderful works."[88]

Just as miracles confirmed the authority and anointing of the ancient prophets and Jesus' apostles, God validates the claims of Jesus through the miracles of the Messiah. Jesus says this very thing repeatedly—that His power is proof that He is the Messiah.

- John 5:36 – …For the works that the Father has given me to accomplish, the very works that I am doing, bear witness about me that the Father has sent me…
- John 10:25 – Jesus answered them, "…The works that I do in my Father's name bear witness about me…"
- John 10:32 – Jesus answered them, "I have shown you many good works from the Father…"
- John 10:36-38 – …do you say of him whom the Father consecrated and sent into the world, "You are blaspheming," because I said, "I am the Son of God"? If I am not doing the works of my Father, then do not believe me; but if I do them, even though you do not believe me, believe the works, that you may know and understand

----

[a] John 21:25

that the Father is in me and I am in the Father.

The preaching of the early Church heralded the miracles of Jesus Christ as evidence of His unprecedented claims to be God and Lord. Jesus' miracles were such a widely known historical fact that Peter said at the launch of the early Church in Acts 2:22, "Men of Israel, hear these words: Jesus of Nazareth, a man attested to you by God with mighty works and wonders and signs that God did through him in your midst, as you yourselves know..." When the Church of Jesus Christ expanded from the Jews to the Gentiles, this same proof of Jesus verified as God through His miracles was preached by Peter in Acts 10:37-39 just before the Holy Spirit fell in divine power: "... you yourselves know what happened...how God anointed Jesus of Nazareth with the Holy Spirit and with power. He went about doing good and healing all who were oppressed by the devil, for God was with him. And we are witnesses of all that he did..." Peter's sermon then proclaims Jesus' greatest miracle of all—rising from death!

Even those who did not convert to worship Jesus recognized His unprecedented supernatural power. Even before he became a Jesus follower, religious leader Nicodemus said of Jesus' miracles, in John 3:2, "Rabbi, we know that you are a teacher come from God, for no one can do these signs that you do unless God is with him." Even the demons cowered in the presence of Jesus' power. Matthew 8:28-29 says that after Jesus calmed a storm by the power of His word, "...two demon-possessed men met him, coming out of the tombs, so fierce that no one could pass that way. And behold, they cried out, 'What have you to do with us, O Son of God? Have you come here to torment us before the time?'"

The Bible opens with a miracle: God creating everyone and everything out of nothing. The pages of the Bible record a parade of miracles until the ultimate miracle occurs: God becoming a man. Then, Jesus Christ performs miracles, including rising from death after atoning for the sin of the world in the greatest miracle of all time.

The Bible uses many terms to denote miracles in the Old

Testament.

> The Old Testament designates certain extraordinary
> phenomena as 'signs' and 'wonders' demonstrating divine
> power. Forms of miracles in the Old Testament include:
> - celestial events (e.g., Josh 10:9–15);
> - instantaneous healings (e.g., 2 Kgs 5:14);
> - control of nature (e.g., Exod 14:21–22);
> - objects and animals acting in unexpected ways (e.g.,
>   Num 22:22–35; 2 Kgs 6:5–7).
>
> The Hebrew Bible frequently portrays God as the direct
> agent of miracles in the Hebrew Bible…"[89]

Because miracles play such a central role in the Scriptures,
numerous words in the original languages are used to explain
these supernatural phenomena.

> The Hebrew words for 'sign'…and 'wonder'… frequently
> refer to miraculous events. While the words typically
> function as synonyms, a sign explicitly notes the referential
> quality of a miracle…The juxtaposition of 'signs' and
> 'wonders' occurs throughout the Hebrew Bible (e.g., Exod
> 7:3; Deut 4:34; 6:22; 7:19; 26:8; 34:11; Isa 8:18; Jer
> 32:20–21..). Three words in the New Testament refer to
> miracles:
> - power…—in certain contexts, "miracle" and "mighty
>   deed" are alternate translations;
> - sign…—often refers to a miracle that figuratively
>   represents something else, such as the kingdom of God
>   or the gospel;
> - wonder…—indicates something extraordinary. The
>   juxtaposition of 'signs' … and 'wonders' …occurs in the
>   New Testament with the combination of the Greek
>   words for 'signs and wonders' … (e.g., Mark 13:22; John
>   4:48; Acts 2:43; Rom 15:19) … John refers to Jesus'
>   miracles as works (e.g., John 10:20) … [and] In the New
>   Testament 'wonder' in the sense of simple amazement (2
>   Cor 11:14; Rev 17:6).[90]

The four Gospels that report Jesus' miracles each do so with a different emphasis.

> Mark's Gospel treats miracles as symbolic demonstrations of the kingdom of God rather than validations of Jesus and the gospel...Matthew's Gospel uses miracles to portray Jesus as the fulfillment of God's promise to raise up a prophet like Moses (Deut 18:18)...Luke's Gospel and Acts refer to the miracles of Jesus and the early Christ-followers as validating signs and wonders (e.g., Acts 2:43)...John's Gospel describes Jesus' miracles as explanatory signs... the text never calls them 'miracles'... [In addition,] Miraculous signs and wonders are confirmations of Paul's apostleship and valuable evangelistic tools (Rom 15:19; 2 Cor 12:12). Paul considers the ability to perform miracles a spiritual gift (1 Cor 12:10, 28–29).[91]

The functions of those miracles include the following:

M – Majesty. God shows up to reveal His divine attributes and demonstrate sovereign power. (Example: Sparing Daniel and his friends from death sentences in a fiery furnace and lions' den.)

I – Increase Faith. God shows up in power to reinvigorate the waning faith of His people. (Example: For instance, the disciples transformed from cowards to courageous upon witnessing Jesus' Resurrection.)

R – Revelation. God speaks a message. (Example: Writing the 10 Commandments on stone, the hand writing on the wall in Daniel, and Jesus speaking to Moses through the burning bush.)

A – Anger. God crushes demonic false gods and other enemies, showing His sovereign power. (Example: Destroying Sodom and Gomorrah, destroying the nation of Egypt and their false gods, or bringing down fire for Elijah.)

C – Care. God provides for the needs of His people. (Example:

Feeding His people in the wilderness during the Exodus or Jesus multiplying the little boy's lunch.)

L – Liberation. God spares His people from devastation. (Example: Parting the Red Sea or removing demonic forces for people to live in full freedom.)

E – Evangelism. God shows up in power to prove He is the One True God, which results in people believing in Him. (Example: When some Egyptians left their nation with God's people after He supernaturally delivered them, or miracles followed by salvations throughout the book of Acts.)

HOW ARE MIRACLES ALSO SIGNS?

For over a decade, we had a smart German shepherd as the family dog. When someone points, most dogs look at the finger rather than in the direction they are pointing. Kaya was a smart dog, and when you would point in a direction, she would look in that direction rather than at your finger.

When it comes to miracles, most people are like the average dog and look at the miracle rather than seeing it as a sign pointing in the direction of the Kingdom of God. Christians are supposed to not just look at the miracles but also look at miracles as signs pointing us to something much bigger—King Jesus and His Kingdom.

Each of Jesus' miracles was a sign pointing to the Kingdom of God. For example, Matthew 9 is a list of miracles with Jesus healing a paralytic, restoring a girl to life, healing a woman, healing two blind men, and healing a mute man unable to speak. He then explains the meaning of these miracles, saying, "And Jesus went throughout all the cities and villages, teaching in their synagogues and proclaiming the gospel of the kingdom and healing every disease and every affliction..."

If you had to guess which was Jesus' first miracle, what would your guess be? If your guess was that Jesus turned water into wine at a wedding, you would have been correct. John 2:1-11 tells the story, which ends by saying, "This, the first of his signs, Jesus did at Cana in Galilee, and manifested his glory. And his disciples believed in him.

Like signs we see when we drive on the road, signs in the Bible are pointing us towards a destination. When Jesus performs a miracle, it is a "sign" pointing to the Kingdom of God. Jesus is clear that a list of miracles is of no use unless you follow where they are pointing—to King Jesus and the Kingdom of God. Matthew 11:20–24 says,

> Then he [Jesus] began to denounce the cities where most of his mighty works had been done, because they did not repent. "Woe to you, Chorazin! Woe to you, Bethsaida! For if the mighty works done in you had been done in Tyre and Sidon, they would have repented long ago in sackcloth and ashes. But I tell you, it will be more bearable on the day of judgment for Tyre and Sidon than for you. And you, Capernaum, will you be exalted to heaven? You will be brought down to Hades. For if the mighty works done in you had been done in Sodom, it would have remained until this day. But I tell you that it will be more tolerable on the day of judgment for the land of Sodom than for you."

Too many people seek miracles and not God. God's people should not be chasing signs and wonders. God's people should be chasing God. When we chase God, we can expect that a few miracles will follow us as we follow Jesus. In Matthew 16:4, Jesus says, "An evil and adulterous generation seeks for a sign..."

Jesus' first miracle is a sign pointing to the Kingdom. In Matthew 22:2-3, Jesus says that weddings are Kingdom signs, saying, "The kingdom of heaven may be compared to a king who gave a wedding feast for his son, and sent his servants to call those who were invited to the wedding feast, but they would not come." Revelation 19:6-9 says history will end with the Wedding Supper of the Lamb when Jesus (like a groom) and the Church (like a bride) are united together forever. Furthermore, on that day God's people will wear white, showing that Jesus has forever made us clean, pure, and blameless in

His sight. It is for this reason that Christian weddings are also supposed to be signs pointing to this event, as the bride wears white no matter what she has done because she is pure in Christ. The presence of fine wine at the wedding in Jesus' day also points to the eternal Kingdom party spoken of in Isaiah 25:6 (NLT): "...the Lord of Heaven's Armies will spread a wonderful feast for all the people of the world. It will be a delicious banquet with clear, well-aged wine and choice meat."

The miracles of God point to the Kingdom of God and Jesus as King of Kings. When we see Jesus healing people, those miracles are signs pointing to the Kingdom when all of God's people will be fully healed forever. When we see Jesus casting demons away from people, those signs point to the Kingdom of God when Satan and demons are banished forever. When Jesus commands nature, we are to look forward to the Kingdom of God, where the curse is lifted, and creation is fully restored. When we see Jesus performing miracles to feed multitudes, those are signs pointing to the Kingdom of God, where all our needs will be met by the grace of our King.

When we see Jesus raising people from the dead, those miracles are signs pointing forward to the resurrection of God's people to be with Him in joy forever! When we see Jesus performing miracles at parties and people throwing parties to celebrate His miracles, those are signs pointing to the eternal Kingdom party that never ends!

Lastly, for those Christians who are reading this and wonder why they have never seen a miracle, I want to encourage you. If you are a Christian, you have experienced a miracle. The only way anyone can become a Christian is by God doing a miracle in your life. Ephesians 2:1-5 says that a non-Christian is

> ...dead in the trespasses and sins... following the prince of the power of the air...by nature children of wrath...But God, being rich in mercy, because of the great love with which he loved us, even when we were dead in our trespasses, made us alive together with Christ—by grace you have been saved...

There's a story in the Bible where a man named Lazarus lay dead for multiple days. Jesus called Lazarus by name, and the dead man returned to life! That is obviously a miracle. What Jesus did for you spiritually is the same as what He did for Lazarus physically. You were spiritually dead and belonged to Satan, then Jesus called your name, and you were born again, given spiritual life, and saved from your former life and the eternal wrath of God! Before you knew God, God knew you. Before you called out to God, God called out to you. For this reason, the testimony of every Christian is a miracle story. God showed up in your life to save you!

The church Father Augustine (A.D. 354-430) believed,

> ...the greatest miracle was the renovation of the heart, the healing of human desire from its corruption so that God is loved above all and one's neighbor as oneself. While not denying "physical miracles," Augustine wrote in *Expositions of the Psalms* that these 'miracles of the soul' were the premier evidence of God's ongoing creative work in the world.[92]

CHAPTER 7
WHAT DID KING JESUS ACCOMPLISH ON THE CROSS?

...God shows his love for us in that while we were still sinners, Christ died for us. –Romans 5:8

Suffering.

What suffering are you experiencing right now? Much of our life is spent trying to avoid suffering, and when we do suffer, we expend great effort seeking to minimize or even eliminate it.

Now, consider how Jesus Christ is completely unlike us. In Heaven, there was no sin or suffering. Jesus left His throne in glory to come into our world where He was poor, despised, opposed, slandered, rejected, and murdered in the most painful way possible.[a]

Tragically, there is a strong attempt to portray Jesus as solely a social-justice warrior by progressives who want to downplay, or even ignore, that we are sinners, and Jesus came primarily to die for sinners. Jesus the Godman taught the foolish, fed the hungry, healed the sick, encouraged the brokenhearted, counseled the wayward, and loved the sinner. Yet, Jesus was emphatic that the primary purpose of His coming to earth was to suffer and die for our sin. In John 12:27–28, which chronicles the week leading up to Jesus' death, He says, "Now is my soul troubled. And what shall I say? 'Father, save me from this hour'? But for this purpose I have come to this hour. Father, glorify your name." In that moment, Jesus was setting His gaze on the cross.

Who would you be willing to suffer and die for? Would you suffer and die for a total stranger? How about an enemy? That is precisely what Jesus did for us on the cross—He willingly suffered and died on the cross for His enemies.

---

[a] On this point, we have a difference of opinions and think it's important to state this, as it's possible to do ministry together with differing opinions on open-handed issues. Mark would say that Jesus experienced the wrath of God on the cross based upon Jesus being "forsaken" (Matthew 27:46; Mark 15:34) and the double imputation of our sin to Jesus and His righteousness to believers (2 Corinthians 5:21). Gerry would say that, like the Passover Lamb, and the first goat on the Day of Atonement, Jesus is the Lamb sacrificed, crushed by the Father (Isaiah 53:10), but He was not personally punished. He would say God's wrath was satisfied by the Substitute rather than falling on the Substitute.

CRUCIFIXION

One Bible dictionary says, "The cross was called the 'infamous stake,' the 'criminal wood,' and the 'most evil cross'…" and "Cicero described crucifixion as 'the cruelest and most terrible punishment'…"[93]

The same Bible dictionary continues,

Precrucifixion torture usually involved flogging, and could also include burning, racking, mutilation, and abuse of the victim's family. Plato (though Greek) describes the general practice in precrucifixion tortures: "[A man] is racked, mutilated, has his eyes burned out, and after having had all sorts of great injuries inflicted on him, and having seen his wife and children suffer the like, is at last impaled (i.e., crucified) or tarred and burned alive" (Plato, *Gorgias* 473bc; translation in Jowett, "Gorgias"). In another text, Plato writes: "The just man who is thought to be unjust will be scourged, racked, bound—will have his eyes burnt out; and, at last after suffering every kind of evil, he will be impaled (i.e., crucified)" (*Republic* 361e–362a; Jowett, *Republic*, 50).[94]

Imagine a long wooden stake being run through a person's midsection, and that stake then being driven into the ground, with the impaled person left to die slowly over the course of many days. It is believed that this kind of barbarous torture may be the earliest form of crucifixion, occurring as early as the ninth century B.C.[95]

In the sixth century B.C., the Persians commonly practiced crucifixion, especially King Darius I, who crucified 3,000 Babylonians in 518 B.C. In 332 B.C., Alexander the Great crucified 2,000 people whom he conquered in Tyre. The transition from impalement to crucifixion occurred under Alexander, as he was a master of terror and dread. In 71 B.C., the former gladiator Spartacus and 120,000 prisoners fell in battle to the Romans, which resulted in 6,000 men being crucified along the shoulder of the highway for 120 miles.

The same murderous spirit of domination, fear, and control continues to be used by evil governments to control their citizens throughout history. Under the leadership of Adolf Hitler, German soldiers crucified Jews at Dachau by running bayonets and knives through their legs, shoulders, throats, and testicles. Under the leadership of Pol Pot, the Khmer Rouge performed crucifixions in Cambodia. Today, crucifixion continues in Sudan. Crucifixion was and is brutal. In recent times, crucifixion continues by extremist terrorist groups such as ISIS. A recent news headline said, "Beheadings, crucifixions and heads on spikes: Inside Saudi Arabia's 'relentless killing spree' of medieval-style executions - including 81 in one day - that has seen record numbers put to death..."[96]

Evil governments publicly torment leaders, including crucifixions, to bring panic to their followers. The message is clear: if you follow this leader, we will punish you with extreme force. This fact makes the explosion and expansion of the Christian Church, despite the public crucifixion of Jesus Christ and His disciples, even more powerful of a testimony that He did not stay dead.

A Bible dictionary describes how those who performed crucifixions often abused the family of the person being crucified:

> Perhaps the cruelest practice was abusing or even executing the victim's family members as he hung on the cross. The Athenians crucified Artayctes by nailing him to a wooden plank; while he was thus fastened, they stoned his son in front of him (Herodotus, *Histories* 9.120; see also 4.202). Alexander Jannaeus, the Jewish high priest and prince, crucified 800 Pharisees and had their wives and children slaughtered in front of them as they hung from the crosses.[97]

The Romans perfected crucifixion: they reserved it as the most painful mode of execution for the most despised people. It was a sign of the power of Rome to crush those who dared oppose them. The crucifixion methods varied with the sadism of the soldiers. They tried to outdo one another and experimented with various forms of torture. They grew in and learned ways to prolong the pain and agony.

Adding to their shame, "[v]ictims were almost always executed without clothing, probably to make them more susceptible to blows and to increase their shame."[98]

A Bible dictionary continues,

Victims could be placed on the cross in several different ways. Seneca wrote: "Some [executioners] hang [their victims] upside down; others drive stakes through the genitals [of the victims]; still others extend [the victims'] arms on the *patibulum*" (Dial. 6.20.3; Latin text in Hengel, *Crucifixion*, 25). Josephus described that, when the Romans crucified large numbers of Jewish rebels in the Jewish War (ad 66–73), they "out of rage and hatred amused themselves by nailing their prisoners in different postures" (*Jewish War* 5.51, trans. Thackeray).[99]

The Romans are believed to be the first to crucify on an actual cross. The Tau was a capital T cross, and the Latin was a lowercase t cross. Both had the stipe (the vertical post) and patibulum (the crossbar). The stipe was probably permanent while each man carried his own patibulum.

As a young boy, Jesus may have viewed crucifixions in Judea. There was a Jewish uprising against the Romans that resulted in the mass crucifixion of about 2,000 Jews in A.D. 4 at the time of the death of Herod.

The pain of crucifixion is so horrendous that a word was invented to explain it— "excruciating"—which literally means "from the cross." The victim was affixed to the cross with either ropes or nails. The pain of crucifixion is due in part to the fact that it is a prolonged and agonizing death by asphyxiation. Crucified people could hang on the cross for anywhere from a few hours to as long as nine days, passing in and out of consciousness as their lungs struggled to breathe while laboring under the weight of their body.

To end the torment, it was not uncommon for those

being crucified to slump on the cross to empty their lungs of air and thereby hasten their death. Further, there are debated archaeological reports that suggest sometimes seats were placed underneath the buttocks of those being crucified to prevent slumping, thereby ensuring a lengthy and most painful death.

None of this was done in dignified privacy, but rather in open, public places. It would be like nailing a bloodied, naked man above the front entrance to your local mall. Crowds would gather around the victims to mock them as they sweated in the sun, bled, and became incontinent from the pain.

Once dead, some victims were not given a decent burial but rather left on the cross for vultures to pick apart from above while dogs chewed on the bones that fell to the ground, even occasionally taking a hand or foot home as a chew toy, according to ancient reports.[100] Whatever remained of the victim would eventually be thrown in the garbage and taken to the dump unless the family buried it. Furthermore, the family kept and reused the wooden crosses and nails, considering them more valuable than the deceased's bodies.

As a general rule, it was men who were crucified at eye level so that passersby could look him directly in the eye as he died. In the rare event of a woman's crucifixion, she was made to face the cross. Not even such a barbarous culture was willing to watch the face of a woman in such excruciating agony. The ancient Jewish historian Josephus called crucifixion "the most wretched of deaths."[101] The ancient Roman philosopher Cicero asked that decent Roman citizens not even speak of the cross because it was too disgraceful a subject for the ears of decent people.[102] The Jews also considered crucifixion the most horrific mode of death, as Deuteronomy 21:22–23 says: "…if a man has committed a crime punishable by death and he is put to death, and you hang him on a tree, his body shall not remain all night on the tree, but you shall bury him the same day, for a hanged man is cursed by God."

In light of all this, perhaps most peculiar is the fact that the symbol for Jesus, which has become the most famous symbol in all of history, is the cross. The church father Tertullian (A.D. 155–230) tells us of the early practice of believers' making the sign of the cross over their bodies with their hands and adorning their necks and homes with crosses to celebrate the brutal death of Jesus. In so doing, the early Christians turned a symbol of terror and intimidation into a symbol of salvation and hope.

HOW CAN JESUS' CRUCIFIXION BE GOOD NEWS?

In the days leading up to His death, Jesus was a healthy young man in His early thirties. Jesus spoke openly of his impending death, including at the Passover meal He ate with His friends as the Last Supper. There, he broke with fifteen centuries of protocol. In so doing, he showed that the Passover meal, which God's people had been eating annually, found its ultimate fulfillment in him. The Passover memorialized the night in Egypt when in faith God's people covered the doorposts of their home with blood so that death would not come to the firstborn son in their home but would rather pass them over.[a] Jesus, the firstborn Son of God, likewise had come to die and cover us with His blood so that God's just wrath would literally pass over us sinners as the essence of the new covenant.[b]

During the Last Supper, Satan entered one of Jesus' disciples, Judas, who had been stealing money from Jesus' ministry and had agreed to hand Him over to the authorities to be crucified. After Judas left the meal to lead the soldiers to Jesus, Jesus went to the garden of Gethsemane, where he spent a sleepless night in the agony of prayer. Meanwhile, His disciples failed to intercede for Him in prayer and instead kept falling asleep. At this point, Jesus was fully aware of His impending crucifixion and was so distressed that, as the Bible records, He sweat drops of blood, a physical condition that doctors report is rare because it requires an elevated level of stress that few people ever experience.

After an exhausting, sleepless night of distress, Judas arrived with the soldiers and betrayed Jesus with a kiss. Jesus

---

[a] Exodus 6-12 [b] Luke 22:19-21

was then arrested. He was forced to walk through a series of false trials where contradicting false witnesses were brought forward to offer false testimony. Despite the absence of any evidence supporting the false charges, Jesus was sentenced to be murdered. He was eventually blindfolded as a mob of cowardly men beat Him mercilessly. He was then stripped in great shame, and the Bible simply says that they had Him scourged.

Scourging itself was such a painful event that many people died from it without even making it to their cross. Jesus' hands would have been chained above His head to expose His back and legs to an executioner's whip called a cat-o'-nine tails or a flagrum. Two men, one on each side, took turns whipping the victim. The whip was a series of long leather straps. At the end of some of the straps were heavy balls of metal intended to tenderize the body of a victim, like a chef tenderizes a steak by beating it. Some of the straps had hooks made of glass, metal, or bone that would have sunk deeply into the shoulders, back, buttocks, and legs of the victim. Once the hooks had lodged into the tenderized flesh, the executioner would rip the skin, muscle, tendons, and even bones off the victim. The victim's skin and muscles would hang off the body like ribbons as the hooks dissected the skin to the nerve layers. The damage could go so deep that even the lungs were bruised, which made breathing difficult. Some doctors have compared the damage of flogging to the results of a shotgun blast.[103] The victim would bleed profusely and would often go into shock due to severe blood loss and insufficient blood flow near and through the heart.

Jesus' bare back and shoulders, though bloodied and traumatized, were then forced to carry His roughly hewn wooden cross to His place of crucifixion. If Jesus carried the entire cross, it would have weighed a few hundred pounds, and many think it is more likely He carried just the crossbar (patibulum), which would have been about 100 pounds.

Despite His young age and good health, Jesus was so physically devastated from His sleepless night, miles of walking, severe beating, and scourging that He collapsed under the weight of the cross, unable to carry it alone. Doctors have said that the trauma from the heavy crossbar crushing His chest into the ground could have caused a bruised heart, similar to the chest trauma caused by a car accident without a seatbelt where the driver is violently thrown against the steering wheel.[104] Understandably unable to continue carrying His cross on the roughly one-mile journey to His execution, a man named Simon of Cyrene was appointed to carry Jesus' cross. Upon arriving at His place of crucifixion, they pulled Jesus' beard out—an act of ultimate disrespect in ancient cultures—spat on Him, and mocked Him in front of His family and friends.

Jesus the carpenter, who had driven many nails into wood with His own hands, then had five to seven-inch rough metal spikes driven into the most sensitive nerve centers on the human body, through His hands and feet. Jesus was nailed to His wooden cross. His body would have twitched involuntarily, writhing in agony.

In further mockery, a sign was posted above Jesus that said, "Jesus of Nazareth, the King of the Jews."[a] A painting later discovered from a second-century Roman graffito further shows the disrespect of Jesus at his crucifixion. The painting depicts the head of a jackass being crucified, with a man standing alongside it with his arms raised. The caption reads, "Alexamenos worships his god."

"In the second century, Celsus attacked Christianity by appealing to the shameful means of Jesus' execution. Another second century pagan author, Lucian of Samosata, called Jesus the 'crucified sophist' (*Death of Peregrinus* 11–13)."[105]

At this point during a crucifixion, the victims labored to breathe as their bodies went into shock. Victims would become so overwhelmed with pain that they would become incontinent, and a pool of sweat, blood, urine, and feces would gather at the base of their cross.

Jesus' crucifixion was a hideously grotesque scene. Hundreds of years in advance, the prophet Isaiah saw it this way:

---

[a] John 19:19

He was despised and rejected by men; a man of sorrows, and acquainted with grief; and as one from whom men hide their faces he was despised, and we esteemed him not. Surely he has borne our griefs and carried our sorrows; yet we esteemed him stricken, smitten by God, and afflicted.[a]

Crucifixion usually kills by asphyxiation in addition to other factors—the heart is deeply stressed, the body is traumatized, the muscles are devastated, and the blood loss is severe. Doctors have thought that Jesus likely had a chest contusion and possibly a bruised heart from falling with the cross on top of him, which caused an aneurysm.[106] Subsequently, Jesus' heart would have been unable to pump enough blood, and His lungs would have filled up with carbon monoxide. Jesus not only lived through all of this, but He even spoke lucidly and clearly with enough volume to be heard by those present.

From the cross, Jesus announced forgiveness for those who crucified Him, assured the criminal crucified next to Him that they would be together in paradise, commended His mother to John, cried of forsakenness showing His spiritual death and separation from the Father, and expressed His agonized thirst.[107]

At last, Jesus said in a loud voice of triumph, "It is finished."[b] At this moment, the death required as payment for sin to satisfy the holiness, righteousness, justice, and wrath of the triune God was complete, paid by our Substitute, Jesus Christ. Jesus then said, "Father, into your hands I commit my spirit!"[c] Jesus reserved His final breath from the cross to shout His triumphant victory to the world by confirming that He had been restored to God the Father after atoning for human sin. The Bible then simply records that Jesus breathed His last and died. Jesus hung on the cross for at least six hours—from the third hour to the ninth hour, when the darkness ended.[d]

Furthermore, to ensure Jesus was dead, a professional executioner ran a spear through His side, which punctured His heart sac, and water and blood flowed from His side. This is further evidence that Jesus died of a heart attack; the sac around

[a] Isa. 53:3-4 [b] John 19:30 [c] Luke 23:46 [d] Mark 15:25,33

the heart filled with water until the pressure caused Jesus' heart to stop beating. Thus, Jesus possibly died with both a literal and metaphorical broken heart.

For many years, the most sacred place on earth had been the temple, where the presence of God dwelled behind a thick curtain. Only one person each year, the high priest, was allowed to pass by that curtain and enter the presence of God on one day, the Day of Atonement. At the death of Jesus, however, the temple curtain was torn from top to bottom, signifying that God had opened His presence to the world through the cross of Jesus.

HOW IS JESUS' CROSS GOOD NEWS?

The most succinct summary of the gospel in Scripture provides insight into this theological meaning: "…that Christ died for our sins in accordance with the Scriptures, that he was buried, that he was raised on the third day in accordance with the Scriptures…"[a] In this packed section of Scripture, Paul appoints the death, burial, and resurrection of Jesus as the most important event in all of history and the verification of the truthfulness of all Scripture.

He then explains why this is good news with the simple word "for," showing that Jesus died "for our sins." The word "for" can mean either "for the benefit of" or "because of." Jesus did not die "for the benefit of" our sins. He did not help them at all! Rather, He died "because of" our sins. So, it was our sins but His death. From the beginning of sacred Scripture[b] to the end[c], the penalty for sin is death. Therefore, if we sin, we should die. But it is Jesus, the sinless one, who dies in our place "for our sins." The good news of the gospel is that Jesus died to take onto Himself the penalty for our sin. In theological terms, this means that Jesus' death was substitutionary, or vicarious, and in our place solely for our benefit and without benefit for Himself. Thus, the cross of Jesus is the crux of good news because Jesus atoned for our sins according to the promises of

----
[a] 1 Cor. 15:3b-4 [b] Gen. 2:17 [c] Rev. 21:8

Scripture.

Jesus' work for us on the cross is called atonement (at-one-ment); Jesus, our God, became a man to restore a relationship between God and humanity. The concept of Jesus' dying in our place to pay our penalty for our sins has been expressed in theological shorthand as penal substitution. Scripture repeatedly and clearly declares that Jesus died as our substitute, paying our penalty "for" our sins.[a]

One theologian has called the cross the great jewel of the Christian faith. Like every great jewel, it has many precious facets that are each worthy of examining for their brilliance and beauty.[108]

Many of these facets were foreshadowed in the Old Testament, specifically by the annual celebration of the Day of Atonement (Yom Kippur) according to the regulations of the book of Leviticus. The Day of Atonement was the most important day of the year and was often referred to simply as "the day." It was intended to deal with the sin problem between humanity and God. Of the many prophetic elements on this special day, one stands out. On that day, they chose two healthy goats without defect, fit to symbolize sinless perfection.

The first goat was a propitiating sin offering. The high priest slaughtered this innocent goat, which acted as a substitute for the sinners who rightly deserved a violently bloody death for their many sins. He then sprinkled some of its blood on the mercy seat on top of the Ark of the Covenant inside the Most Holy Place. The goat was no longer innocent when it took the guilt of sin; it was a sin offering for the people.[b] Subsequently, its blood represented life given as payment for sin. The dwelling place of God was thus cleansed of the defilement that resulted from all the transgressions and sins of the people of Israel, and God's just and holy wrath was satisfied.

Then the high priest, acting as the representative and mediator between the sinful people and their holy God, would take the second goat and lay his hands on the animal

---

[a] Isa. 53:5, 12; Rom. 4:25; 5:8; Gal. 3:13; 1 Pet. 3:18; 1 John 2:2 [b] Lev. 16:15

while confessing the sins of the people. This goat, called the scapegoat, would then be sent away to run free into the wilderness away from the sinners, symbolically expiating our sins by taking them away.

These great images of the priest, slaughter, and scapegoat are all given by God to help us more fully comprehend Jesus' work for us on the cross, which we will now examine in depth.

HOW DOES GOD SATISFY HIMSELF THROUGH THE CROSS?

New-Covenant Sacrifice

One scholar says that blood is mentioned some 362 times in the Old Testament and some 92 times in the New Testament, even more often than the cross or death of Jesus; thus, it is the most common means by which the Scriptures refer to the death of Jesus.

Throughout Scripture, blood is connected with punishment for sin. Leviticus 17:11 says, "For the life of the flesh is in the blood, and I have given it for you on the altar to make atonement for your souls, for it is the blood that makes atonement by the life." Blood is sacred, epitomizing the life of the sacrificial victim given as a substitute for the sinner's death. Practically every sacrifice included the sprinkling or smearing of blood on an altar, thus teaching that atonement involves the substitution of life for life.

One of the major functions of the Old Testament temple was the slaughtering of animals, as seen by the stream of blood that often flowed out of the temple. Blood is, in fact, a major aspect of Old Testament religion. There were some 11 different sacrifices that fit into one of four groupings (burnt, peace, sin, or guilt), and sacrifices were made both in the morning and evening, all of which involved blood.

This theme of blood, like every theme of Scripture, finds its fulfillment in the coming of Jesus Christ into human history. Early in Jesus' life, His cousin John saw Jesus coming and declared, "Behold, the Lamb of God, who takes away the sin of the world!"[a] This, of course, would be accomplished by Jesus' death on the cross, where His blood flowed freely.

The results of Jesus' shed blood are staggering. Hebrews 9:22 says, "Indeed, under the law almost everything is purified with blood, and without the shedding of blood there is no forgiveness of sins." Also, 1 Peter 1:18–19 says, "You were ransomed from the futile ways inherited from your forefathers, not with perishable things such as silver or gold, but with the precious blood of Christ, like that of a lamb without blemish or spot."

Propitiation

The more we know what is going on in this world, the angrier and more frustrated we become. Imagine, for a moment, what it must be like to be God. Every moment of every day, God sees, hears, knows, and feels all the evil and injustice occurring constantly across our entire planet. God getting angry at evil is not a bad thing; in fact, God gets angry at evil precisely because He is good.

The Bible is filled with examples of God getting angry at sinners and of His anger as hostile, burning, and furious.[b] Because God is holy, good, and just, He not only feels angry about sin but also deals with it in ways that are holy, good, and just. Because God is perfect, His anger is perfect and, as such, is aroused slowly[c], sometimes turned away[d], often delayed[e], and frequently held back.[f]

God's anger is not limited to the Old Testament. Even Jesus got angry, furious, and enraged.[g] Also, Revelation 19 reveals Jesus coming again as a warrior riding on a white horse to slaughter evildoers until their blood runs through the streets like a river.

Furthermore, God feels angry because God hates sin.[h] Sadly, it is commonly said among Christians that "God hates the sin but loves the sinner." This comes from the Hindu Gandhi, who coined the phrase "Love the sinner but hate the

---

[a] John 1:29 [b] Lev. 26:27-30; Num. 11:1; Deut. 29:24 [c] Ex. 34:6-8 [d] Deut. 13:17 [e] Isa. 48:9 [f] Ps. 78:38 [g] Mark 3:5 [h] Prov. 6:16-19; Zech. 8:17

sin" in his 1929 autobiography.

Additionally, God's anger at sin and hatred of sinners causes Him to pour out His wrath on unrepentant sinners. This doctrine is not as popular among professing Christians in our day as it was in past times, but the fact remains that, in the Old Testament alone, nearly 20 words are used for God's wrath, which is spoken of roughly 600 times. The wrath of God also appears roughly 25 times in the New Testament.[a]

The truth is that everyone except the sinless Jesus merits the active wrath of God. None of us deserves love, grace, or mercy from God. Demons and sinful people who fail to repent will have God's wrath burning against them forever.[b] The place of God's unending active wrath is Hell.

However, God's wrath is diverted from some people because of the mercy of God. This is made possible because of the cross, where Jesus substituted Himself in our place for our sins and appeased God's righteous wrath. Two sections of Scripture speak to this matter pointedly:

1. Romans 5:9 – Since, therefore, we have now been justified by his blood, much more shall we be saved by him [Jesus] from the wrath of God.
2. 1 Thessalonians 1:9-10 – …you turned to God from idols to serve the living and true God, and to wait for his Son from heaven, whom he raised from the dead, Jesus who delivers us from the wrath to come.

Scripture also has a single word to designate how Jesus diverts the active wrath of our rightfully angry God from us so that we are loved and not hated. That word is *propitiation*, which summarizes more than 600 related words and events that explain it. The word propitiation appears four times in the New Testament.[c] An academic Bible word study book says,

When the New Testament speaks of "propitiation," it means that Jesus' death on the cross for the sins of mankind

---

[a] John 3:36; Eph. 5:6; Col. 3:6; 1 Thess. 1:9-10 [b] Deut. 32:21-22; John 3:36; Eph. 5:6; 2 Pet. 2:4; Rev. 14:9-11 [c] Romans 3:23-25; Hebrews 2:17; 1 John 2:2; 1 John 4:10

appeased God's wrath against His people once and for all. 1 John 4:10 states that God demonstrated His love to us by sending His Son to become "the propitiation for our sins." Just as in the Old Testament God met with His people when the blood of the sin offering was sprinkled on the altar, so Christ's death brings us into fellowship with God.[109]

Furthermore, God's wrath will remain on those who reject Jesus' propitiation. John 3:36 says, "Whoever believes in the Son has eternal life; whoever does not obey the Son shall not see life, but the wrath of God remains on him."

Justification

When something wrong is done to us, be it illegal or immoral, the conscience God placed within us cries out for justice. Through the cross of Jesus Christ, God made a way for Him to receive justice and us to receive grace.

How can a holy God maintain relationship with unholy people? The answer is justification: guilty sinners can be declared righteous before God, that is forgiven of sin before God and accepted as His children by grace alone through faith alone because of the person and work of Jesus Christ alone. Justification is mentioned more than 200 times in various ways throughout the New Testament alone.

The penalty of sin is death. God warned Adam in the garden that "in the day that you eat of it you shall surely die."[a] Paul confirms this saying, "...they know God's righteous decree that those who practice such things deserve to die..."[b] The amazing truth is that God Himself, the second person of the Trinity, paid our debt of death in our place.

Additionally, not only did Jesus take all our sins (past, present, and future) on the cross, but He also gave to us his perfect righteousness as a faultless and sinless person. 1 Corinthians 1:30 says to Christians, "And because of him

---

[a] Gen. 2:17 [b] Rom. 1:32

you are in Christ Jesus, who became to us wisdom from God, righteousness and sanctification and redemption…"

There is absolutely nothing we can do to contribute to our justification. When Jesus said, "It is finished" on the cross, the substitutionary death that needed to be done for our justification was completed in Him. He then took His blood into the heavenly temple to complete the propitiatory work.[a] Titus 3:7 speaks of "being justified by his grace…" Furthermore, Romans 5:16–17 says,

> …the free gift is not like the result of that one man's [Adam's] sin. For the judgment following one trespass brought condemnation, but the free gift following many trespasses brought justification. For if, because of one man's trespass, death reigned through that one man, much more will those who receive the abundance of grace and the free gift of righteousness reign in life through the one man Jesus Christ.

To be justified means to trust only in the person and work of Jesus and no one and nothing else as the object of our faith, righteousness, and justification before God.[b]

Gift Righteousness

Jesus said, "…unless your righteousness exceeds that of the scribes and Pharisees, you will never enter the kingdom of heaven."[c] No one had been more religiously devoted than the Pharisees. Jesus' point is that God is perfectly holy, and Heaven is a perfectly holy place, which requires only perfectly holy people be allowed into His presence forever. This is impossible for sinners, even the best behaved, and requires Jesus to take our sin and give us His holy righteousness.

On the cross, what the Protestant Reformer Martin Luther liked to call the "great exchange" occurred. Jesus took our sin and gave us His righteousness. 2 Corinthians 5:21 says, "For

----

[a] Hebrews 9:12 [b] Acts 13:38; Rom. 4:3-5; 5:1 [c] Matt. 5:20

our sake he [God] made him [Jesus] to be sin who knew no sin, so that in him we might become the righteousness of God." Unlike the self-righteousness of religion, gift righteousness is not something we bring to God to impress Him, but rather something that God does for us and in us, and we receive as a gift by personal faith in Jesus Christ alone. Gift righteousness gives us a new identity as a child of God, a new nature through new birth, a new power by the indwelling Holy Spirit, and a new community, the church.

The gifted righteousness of Jesus is imparted to us at the time of faith, simultaneous with our justification. Not only does God give us family status, but He also gives us new power and a new heart through the indwelling Holy Spirit. This is what theologians call regeneration, or being "born again." Therefore, we not only have a new status of family members by virtue of being justified, but we also have a new heart from which new desires for holiness flow and a new power through God the Holy Spirit to live like, for, and with Jesus as He works for us, in us, and through us. The result is that the Christian life is not a list of things that we have to do (e.g. read the Bible, pray, obey God, worship in church) but instead gifts we get to do because, as a new person with new desires, we want to live out of the righteousness gifted to us by Jesus Christ. That is the basis of our life as His disciples who "say 'No' to ungodliness and worldly passions, and to live self-controlled, upright and godly lives in this present age, while we wait for the blessed hope–the appearing of the glory of our great God and Savior, Jesus Christ...a people that are his very own, eager to do what is good."[a]

Ransom

People are aware of their financial debt to lenders. What most people are not nearly as aware of is their financial debt to the Lord. God made us to love, honor, and obey Him in thought, word, and deed. Every time we fail to do that

----

[a] Titus 2:12-14, NIV

perfectly, we accrue a debt to God. Every person has sinned against God, and Hell is the eternal prison for spiritual debtors who have stolen from God by living sinful lives. Like all debtors, we need a plan if we hope to pay this debt off.

First, we need a mediator to stand between us and God to establish our total debt and come up with a resolution that God the Father, to whom we are indebted, will find acceptable. 1 Timothy 2:5 (NIV) says, "For there is one God, and there is one mediator between God and mankind, the man Christ Jesus..."[a]

Second, we need a redeemer willing to intercede for us and pay our debt to God. A redeemer is a person who pays the debt of someone else. Titus 2:13-14 speaks of "our great God and Savior Jesus Christ, who gave himself for us to redeem us..." Galatians 3:13 says, "Christ redeemed us from the curse of the law by becoming a curse for us..." Because our sins are against God, only God can forgive our debt of sin. Jesus is God who paid our debt on the cross in order to forgive our sin.[b]

Third, we need a ransom, or a repayment sufficient enough to erase our debt to God. The problem, though, is that our sins are against a completely holy and perfect God and therefore require a perfect payment. Referring to Himself in Mark 10:45, Jesus said, "For even the Son of Man came not to be served but to serve, and to give his life as a ransom for many." 1 Timothy 2:5-6 also speaks of "the man Christ Jesus, who gave himself as a ransom..."

Consider, for a moment, how happy you would be if someone paid off all of your past and current debts in full at no cost to you and promised to also cover all future debts. Spiritually speaking, this is precisely what happened when Jesus Christ died on the cross to pay your past, present, and future debt to God in full!

---

[a] see also Heb. 9:15; 12:24 [b] Matt. 26:63-53; Mark 2:5; John 6:41-58; 8:46; 58-59; 10:30-33; 11:25; 14:6,8-9; 16:28

HOW DOES GOD REDEEM US THROUGH THE CROSS?

Redemption

Sinners are captives, or slaves, held in bondage. 2 Peter 2:19 says, "For whatever overcomes a person, to that he is enslaved." Any person who has tried to obey every commandment in the Bible will say they cannot because they are slaves to sin and not free to be fully holy.

Redemption is synonymous with being liberated, freed, or rescued from bondage and slavery. The word and its derivatives (e.g., redeemer, redeem) appear roughly 150 times in the English Bible, with roughly 20 occurrences in the New Testament.

The prototype for redemption is the Exodus, where God crushed the false god, Pharoah, and set His people free. Exodus 6:6 says, "I am the LORD, and I will bring you out from under the burdens of the Egyptians, and I will deliver you from slavery to them, and I will redeem you with an outstretched arm and with great acts of judgment."[a]

The theme of God the Redeemer echoes throughout the Old Testament.[b] Even before Jesus' birth, it was prophesied that He was God coming into human history to redeem sinners from slavery.[c] At the birth of Jesus, it was prophesied that He is God the Redeemer.[d] Paul often spoke of Jesus as our redeemer: "Jesus Christ . . . gave himself for us to redeem us" and "Redemption . . . is in Christ Jesus."[e] Many more examples of Jesus being offered as the redeemer of slaves are scattered throughout the New Testament.[f]

When Jesus was crucified and His blood was shed, He suffered and died in our place for our sins so that we could be redeemed.[g] Jesus has redeemed us from the curse of the law[h], Satan and demons[i], our sinful flesh[j], and sin.[k] Furthermore, Jesus has redeemed us to eternal life with God[l], and a glorified

---

[a] See also Ex. 15:1–18; Deut. 7:8; 15:15; 2 Sam. 7:23; 1 Chron. 17:21; Isa. 51:10; Mic. 6:4 [b] Ps. 78:35; Isa. 44:24; 47:4; 48:17; 63:16; Jer. 50:34; Hos. 7:13; 13:14 [c] Luke 1:68; 2:38 [d] Ibid. [e] Rom. 3:24; Titus 2:13–14; see also 1 Cor. 1:30; Gal. 3:13–14; 4:4–5; Eph. 1:7 [f] 1 Cor. 1:30; Gal. 3:13–14; 4:4–5; Eph. 1:7 [g] 1 Pet. 1:18–19 [h] Gal. 3:13 [i] Col. 1:13–14 [j] Rom. 6:6–12 [k] Gal. 6:14–15 [l] Ps. 49:15

resurrection body.[a]

HOW DOES GOD TRIUMPH THROUGH THE CROSS?

Christus Victor

Scripture clearly says that there is a very real war between Jesus and the angels and Satan and the demons; sinners have been taken as captives in war.[b] In Luke 4:18, Jesus said, "He has sent me to proclaim liberty to the captives...to set at liberty those who are oppressed..."

There is no way that Satan would release us from his captivity and no way that we could liberate ourselves. Therefore, Jesus came as our triumphant warrior and liberator. Colossians 2:13–15 says,

> ...you, who were dead in your trespasses and the uncircumcision of your flesh, God made alive together with him, having forgiven us all our trespasses, by canceling the record of debt that stood against us with its legal demands. This he set aside, nailing it to the cross. He disarmed the rulers and authorities and put them to open shame, by triumphing over them in him.

Matthew 28:18 says Jesus has all authority now, which means that Satan has no authority over Christians. Christians can now live out Colossians 1:10–14 and

> ...walk in a manner worthy of the Lord, fully pleasing to him, bearing fruit in every good work and increasing in the knowledge of God...He has delivered us from the domain of darkness and transferred us to the kingdom of his beloved Son, in whom we have redemption, the forgiveness of sins.

The Bible uses the word grace to explain the victory Jesus

----

[a] Rom. 8:23 [b] Col. 1:13; 2 Tim. 2:25-26

achieved for us on the cross because there is no logical reason that God would love us and die in our place to liberate us from captivity to Satan, sin, and death, other than His wonderful nature.

Expiation

Consider, for a moment, all the time and energy you put into cleaning yourself and the things in your life. Now consider this question: how do you clean your soul?

In Scripture, some dozen words are used to speak of sin in terms of staining our soul, defiling us, and causing us to be filthy or unclean.[a] The effect of sin, particularly sins committed against us, is that we are dirty. The Bible mentions several causes for our defilement, such as any sin at all, as well as involvement with false religions and/or the occult[b], violence[c], and especially sexual sin.[d]

Our souls are stained and defiled by the filth of sins that we commit and that others commit against us as well as by sin done in our relational presence. In Scripture, places[e], objects (such as the marriage bed)[f], and people are defiled by sin.[g] The Bible is filled with people who were ritually unclean and not to be touched or associated with. The commandments for ceremonial washings and such foreshadow the cleansing power of the death of Jesus.

Through the cross, Jesus Christ has taken our sin away forever, as was foreshadowed by the scapegoat on the Day of Atonement. This goat was sent away to run free into the wilderness, symbolically taking the people's sins with it. Theologically, we call this the doctrine of *expiation*, whereby our sin is expiated or taken away so that we are made clean through Jesus, who is our scapegoat.

The Bible uses words such as atonement, cleansing, and purifying fountain that washes away our defilement and shame to explain how Jesus gives us a new identity as clean.

---

[a] E.g., Ps. 106:39; Prov. 30:11–12; Mark 7:20 [b] Lev. 19:31; Ezek. 14:11 [c] E.g., Lam. 4:14 [d] Gen. 34:5; Lev. 21:14; Num. 5:27; 1 Chron. 5:1 [e] Lev. 18:24–30; Num. 35:34 [f] Heb. 13:4 [g] Genesis 34

- For on this day shall atonement be made for you to cleanse you. You shall be clean before the LORD from all your sins.[a]
- I will cleanse them from all the guilt of their sin against me, and I will forgive all the guilt of their sin and rebellion against me.[b]
- "On that day there shall be a fountain opened…to cleanse them from sin and uncleanness…"[c]

Because a Christian is clean in Christ, they do not need to be ashamed of their past any longer because it is forgiven by Christ and was buried with Christ. Hebrews 12:1–2 says, "…let us run with endurance the race that is set before us, looking to Jesus, the founder and perfecter of our faith, who for the joy that was set before him endured the cross, despising the shame, and is seated at the right hand of the throne of God."

With our filth cleansed and shame lifted, 1 John 1:7–9 says,

> …if we walk in the light, as he is in the light, we have fellowship with one another, and the blood of Jesus his Son cleanses us from all sin. If we say we have no sin, we deceive ourselves, and the truth is not in us. If we confess our sins, he is faithful and just to forgive us our sins and to cleanse us from all unrighteousness.

Jesus does both take away the guilt of our sins and "cleanse us from all unrighteousness" that is the defilement and shame that sin brings on us, and places us in the church to help us walk in purity while helping others do the same. The beauty of this truth of the expiating or cleansing work of Jesus is shown in symbolic acts throughout Scripture, including ceremonial washings[d], baptism[e], and the wearing of white in eternity as a continual reminder of the expiating work of Jesus.[f]

---

[a] Lev. 16:30 [b] Jer. 33:8 [c] Zech. 13:1 [d] Ex. 19:10 [e] Acts 22:16 [f] Rev. 19:7-8

HOW DOES GOD INSPIRE US THROUGH THE CROSS?

Christus Exemplar

Jesus died for our sins, thereby enabling us to experience new life. Jesus lived as our example, showing us what it means to live a truly holy human life. Throughout Jesus' life, He repeatedly stated that the purpose of His life on earth was to glorify God the Father or to make the Father's character visible. Jesus glorifying God the Father included dying on the cross.[a]

At the cross of Jesus, we see that to be like Jesus means that we pick up our cross and follow Him as He commanded.[b] Practically, this means that we glorify God by allowing hardship, pain, and loss to make us more and more like Jesus and give us a more credible witness for Jesus. We rejoice not in the pain but rather in what it can accomplish for the gospel so that something as costly as suffering is not wasted but used for God's glory, our joy, and others' good.

To suffer well—that is, in a way that is purposeful for the progress of the gospel both in and through us—we must continually remember Jesus' cross. Peter says,

> ...what credit is it if, when you sin and are beaten for it, you endure? But if when you do good and suffer for it you endure, this is a gracious thing in the sight of God. For to this you have been called, because Christ also suffered for you, leaving you an example, so that you might follow in his steps. He committed no sin, neither was deceit found in his mouth. When he was reviled, he did not revile in return; when he suffered, he did not threaten, but continued entrusting himself to him who judges justly. He himself bore our sins in his body on the tree, that we might die to sin and live to righteousness. By his wounds you have been healed.[c]

When we are suffering, we can look to Jesus as our example

---

[a] John 12:23, 27-28; 13:30-32; 17:1 [b] Matt. 16:24 [c] 1 Pet. 2:20–24

of how to do so in way that glorifies God and ministers to others, just as He did.

WHAT DOES THE DOCTRINE OF THE CROSS REVEAL ABOUT GOD'S LOVE?

On the cross, Jesus revealed to us the love of God:

- John 3:16 – For God so loved the world, that he gave his only Son, that whoever believes in him should not perish but have eternal life.
- John 15:13 – Greater love has no one than this, that someone lays down his life for his friends.
- Romans 5:8 – ...but God shows his love for us in that while we were still sinners, Christ died for us.
- 1 John 4:9-10 – In this the love of God was made manifest among us, that God sent his only Son into the world, so that we might live through him. In this is love, not that we have loved God but that he loved us and sent his Son to be the propitiation for our sins.

At the cross, we see that the love of God is not merely sentimental but also efficacious. When people speak of love, they usually mean an emotional love that feels affectionate but may not do anything to help. Thankfully, God does not merely feel loving toward us; His love actually compels Him to act on our behalf so that we can be changed by His love.

Through the cross, Jesus took away our sin so that we could be lovingly reconciled to God.[a] Thankfully, God not only graciously takes away our sin but mercifully extends Himself to us, knowing that we desperately need Him.[b]

The cross is something done by you. You murdered God incarnate. The cross is something done for you. God loves you and He died to forgive you.

Through the cross and empty tomb of Jesus Christ, there are at least nine ways that God has loved you by Jesus taking

_____
[a] Isa. 59:2; Hos. 5:6 [b] Isa. 59:2; Hos. 5:6

your place and putting you in His place.

1. Jesus died so you can live!
2. Jesus paid the ultimate price for your debt to God!
3. Jesus was cursed so you could be blessed!
4. Jesus became unrighteous so you could become righteous!
5. Jesus endured God's wrath so you could experience God's grace!
6. Jesus was rejected by the Father so you could be reconciled to the Father!
7. Jesus was shamed so that you could be unashamed!
8. Jesus became unclean to make you clean!
9. Jesus was hated so you could be loved!

CHAPTER 8

DID KING JESUS REALLY RISE FROM DEATH?

Jesus said... "I am the resurrection and the life. Whoever believes in me, though he die, yet shall he live, and everyone who lives and believes in me shall never die." –John 11:25-26

What happens after we die? That question has been the focus of every generation, especially when someone we love dies, or we are facing our own mortality. While other religions, philosophies, and spiritualities speculate about what awaits us on the other side of this life, only Christianity claims to have a certain hope.

Why?

Jesus Christ said He would die, be buried, and, three days later, rise in victory over death. He is the only major religious leader to conquer death, and, to this day, the majority of people believe He rose from death. According to a Rasmussen poll, 68% of people believe Jesus physically rose from the dead, versus 13% who do not believe.[110]

Defining what resurrection does and does not mean is incredibly important. Resurrection does not mean revived, when someone who dies comes back to life only to die again, as happens throughout Scripture.[a] Unlike being revived, resurrection teaches that someone dies and returns to physical life forever, never to die again, or what the Bible calls eternal life[b], patterned after Jesus' death and Resurrection[c].

Resurrection does not mean there is a second chance for salvation after death, as both reincarnation and postmortem salvation wrongly purport. *Reincarnation* is the wrongful belief that the human soul individually migrates from one body to another through a succession of lives in pursuit of complete purification, where the soul is finally joined to the ultimate reality of the divine. *Postmortem salvation* wrongly teaches that God pursues people beyond the boundary of death to be sure they have had a real opportunity to respond to the gospel. Hebrews 9:27 refutes both errors, saying, "...it is appointed for man to die once, and after that comes judgment."

Resurrection does not mean that everyone, believers

---

[a] E.g., 2 Kings 4:18–37; Matt. 9:18–26; 27:52–53; Mark 5:22–43; Luke 8:40–56; John 11:1–44; Acts 9:36–42; 20:9–12 [b] E.g., John 5:24 [c] 1 Corinthians 15

and unbelievers alike, avoids Hell. Universalism wrongly teaches that everyone is eventually saved and goes to Heaven. Annihilationism wrongly teaches that at some point following death, unbelievers simply cease to exist rather than going to an eternal Hell, eternal, personal separation from God. Daniel 12:2 declares that both believers and unbelievers will rise, and some will go to everlasting Heaven and others to everlasting Hell, which refutes both errors: "...many of those who sleep in the dust of the earth shall awake, some to everlasting life, and some to shame and everlasting contempt."

Resurrection does not mean what is called "soul sleep," where both the body and the spirit lie at rest until the resurrection, as is taught by some Seventh Day Adventists. When the New Testament speaks of believers as "asleep," it does so as a metaphor to distinguish the death of believers from the death of unbelievers. A Bible Dictionary says, "The Bible also uses sleep as a metaphor for the death of the righteous. 'Christ has indeed been raised from the dead, the firstfruits of those who have fallen asleep.'[a] In Christ, death is nothing more than a nap from which the righteous will awaken to endless day."[111] This is why Paul speaks of his death as gain, because it means his soul goes to be with Jesus: "For to me to live is Christ, and to die is gain."[b]

Neither does resurrection simply mean life after death. This is because life after death does not initially include the physical body; rather, the body lies in the ground while the spiritual soul goes to be with God. Paul speaks of believers being "away from the body and at home with the Lord."[c]

WHAT IS RESURRECTION?

- Step 1: Living as a whole person, with unified body and spirit.
- Step 2: Die with your body going into the ground and your soul going before the Lord for judgment.
- Step 3: Return to life with your glorified body and soul

---

[a] 1 Cor 15:20 [b] Phil. 1:21 [c] 2 Cor. 5:8

reunited to never die again.

The Bible teaches that we are both a material body and an immaterial soul. Upon death, these two parts are separated.

In Step 1, for the believer, our body goes into the ground and our soul goes to be with God. 2 Corinthians 5:8 says this is being away from the body and at home with the Lord as a precursor to the Kingdom of God, or what the Bible often simply calls Heaven. In Step 2, for the believer, our body and soul are resurrected, we stand before Jesus Christ for a judgment of eternal rewards, and we enter into the Kingdom of God for perfect eternal life.

In Step 1, for the unbeliever, their soul goes to a place called by such names in the Bible as a "prison"[a] and "Death and Hades."[b] That place is a place of just temporary suffering for unbelievers and a precursor to Hell. In Step 2, for unbelievers, they are resurrected from the dead to stand before Jesus and are sentenced to the conscious eternal torments of Hell with complete justice. Revelation 20:13-14 calls this the "second death," saying, "And the sea gave up the dead who were in it, Death and Hades gave up the dead who were in them, and they were judged, each one of them, according to what they had done. Then Death and Hades were thrown into the lake of fire. This is the second death, the lake of fire." While there are different degrees of punishment in Hell[c], all who die without accepting God's gracious forgiveness in Jesus will be forever apart from Him under the penalty of their sin.

Jesus explains the intermediate state where we all live in our soul following death until we experience resurrection. In Luke 16:19-31, Jesus talks about two men referred to as the Rich Man and Lazarus, the poor man, who die, and where they go afterwards. He says, "The poor man died and was carried by the angels to Abraham's side. The rich man also died and was buried, and in Hades, being in torment..." In Jesus' story, although both men die and are living in their not-yet-resurrected soul, there is a "great chasm" or separation that

---

[a] 1 Pet. 3:19 [b] Luke 16:19-31; Revelation 6:8, 20:13-14 [c] Matt. 11:20

"none may cross" showing a person cannot be saved after death. On one side of the "great chasm" is the unbelieving rich man in the place of "anguish," "flame," "Hades," and "place for torment," which is a precursor to the Second Death and Hell following the resurrection. On the other side of the "great chasm" is the believing Lazarus and is called "Abraham's side," where he was "carried by the angels." Since Abraham is the father of faith throughout Scripture, the picture is that all who die with faith in Jesus Christ are at his side in Heaven, ministered to by God's holy angels.

While we correctly say believers go to Heaven when they die, that is to be with Jesus, we must add that our eternal home is on the New Earth as whole persons in a resurrected body. Heaven is our intermediate state in our soul, and the Kingdom of God is our eternal state when in we live forever in our soul and resurrected, perfected, glorified physical body.

WHAT WERE ANCIENT NON-CHRISTIAN VIEWS OF THE AFTERLIFE?

It is commonly purported by some that the entire idea of a bodily resurrection was, in fact, not a novel idea but one borrowed from other ancient philosophies and spiritualities. This is simply not the case.

The most academic and painstaking study of ancient beliefs about bodily resurrection resulted in the 700-page masterpiece from N.T. Wright, *The Resurrection of the Son of God*. Wright undertook a painstakingly exhaustive and revolutionary study of ancient beliefs regarding resurrection. Wright concludes, "In so far as the ancient non-Jewish world had a Bible, its Old Testament was Homer. And in so far as Homer has anything to say about resurrection, he is quite blunt: it doesn't happen."[112]

The idea of resurrection is denied in ancient paganism from Homer all the way to the Athenian dramatist Aeschylus, who wrote, "Once a man has died, and the dust has soaked up his blood, there is no resurrection."[113] Wright provides a helpful summary: "Christianity was born into a world where its central claim was known to be false. Many believed that the dead were non-existent; outside Judaism, nobody believed in resurrection."[114]

One of the most influential writers in antiquity was Plato, who taught dualism—the belief that human beings are two parts. The physical part of us is undesirable, and the spiritual part of us is desirable. The entire goal of ancient Greek philosophy was to die, shed the body, and live solely as a spiritual being. Not only did they not believe in a physical resurrection, but they also considered the entire concept taken from the Old Testament as undesirable and abhorrent.

This view is also evident in the writings of Cicero: "Cicero is quite clear, and completely in the mainstream of Greco-Roman thought: the body is a prison-house. A necessary one for the moment; but nobody in their right mind, having got rid of it, would want it or something like it back again."[115]

After surveying ancient pagan writers and philosophers, Wright concludes, "Nobody in the pagan world of Jesus' day and thereafter actually claimed that somebody had been truly dead and had then come to be truly, and bodily, alive once more."[116]

Furthermore, not even Judaism believed in the resurrection of an individual from death in the middle of history. Their belief was that their entire nation alone would rise from death together at the end of history. Philosopher William Lane Craig's lengthy studies of the Resurrection of Jesus Christ culminated in the publishing of two scholarly books on the issue.[117] Craig asserts,

> Jewish belief always concerned a resurrection at the end of the world, not a resurrection in the middle of history... The resurrection to glory and immortality did not occur until after God had terminated world history. This traditional Jewish conception was the prepossession of Jesus' own disciples (Mark 9:9–13; John 11:24). The notion of a genuine resurrection occurring prior to God's bringing about the world's end would have been foreign to them...Jewish belief always concerned a general resurrection of the people, not the resurrection of an

isolated individual [e.g. Jesus Christ].[118]

Noted historian and professor Edwin Yamauchi, who has immersed himself in 22 languages, ancient archaeology, and history says that there is no possibility that the idea of a resurrection was borrowed by Christians from pagans because there is no definitive evidence for the teaching of a deity resurrection in any of the mystery religions prior to the second century. Apparently, the pagans stole the idea of resurrection from the Christians, and not vice versa.[119] For example, the resurrection of the mythical Greek God Adonis is not spoken of until the second to fourth centuries.[120] Attis, the consort of Cybele, is not referred to as a resurrected god until after A.D. 150.[121]

Some have postulated that the taurobolium ritual of ancient gods Attis and Mithra is the source of the biblical concept of the resurrection. In this ritual, the initiate was put in a pit, and a bull was slaughtered on a grating over him, drenching him with blood. However, the earliest this ritual is mentioned is A.D. 160, and the belief that it led to rebirth is not mentioned until the fourth century. Princeton scholar Bruce Metzger has argued that the taurobolium was said to have the power to confer eternal life only after it encountered Christianity.[122]

The myths of pagans are admittedly fictitious events centered on the annual death and rebirth of vegetation and harvest cycles. Conversely, the Resurrection of Jesus Christ is put forth as a historical fact in a place, at a time, with eyewitnesses and numerable lines of compelling evidence. Furthermore, not only is the theory that Christianity borrowed the concept of resurrection untrue, but it also completely ignores the historical facts of the empty tomb and post-Resurrection appearances of Jesus Christ.

WHAT IS THE BIBLICAL EVIDENCE FOR JESUS' RESURRECTION?

The biblical evidence for Jesus' Resurrection is compelling

and can be briefly summarized in 10 points. Each of these points is consistent, and together they prove that the Bible is emphatically and repeatedly clear on the fact of Jesus' Resurrection.

1. *Jesus' Resurrection was prophesied in advance.* Roughly 700 years before Jesus' birth, the prophet Isaiah promised that Jesus would be born into humble circumstances to live a simple life, die a brutal death, and then rise to take away our sin.[a]

2. *Jesus predicted His Resurrection.* On numerous occasions, Jesus plainly promised that He would die and rise three days later.[b]

3. *Jesus died.* Before Jesus died, He underwent a sleepless night of trials and beatings that left Him exhausted. He was then scourged—a punishment so horrendous that many men died from it before even making it to their crucifixion. Jesus was crucified, and a professional executioner declared Him dead. To ensure Jesus was dead, a spear was thrust through His side, and a mixture of blood and water poured out of His side because the spear burst His heart sac.[c] Jesus' dead body was wrapped in upwards of 100 pounds of linens and spices, which, even if He was able to somehow survive the beatings, floggings, crucifixion, and a pierced heart, would have killed Him by asphyxiation. Even if, through all of this, Jesus somehow survived (which would in itself be a miracle), He could not have endured three days without food, water, or medical attention in a cold tomb carved out of rock, rolled the large stone away guarding the entrance, overwhelmed the Roman soldiers on guard, walked back in to town, and convinced everyone that He was fully healed. In summary, Jesus died.

4. *Jesus was buried in a tomb that was easy to find.* Some 700

---

[a] Isa. 53:8-12 [b] Isa. 53:8-12 [c] John 19:34–35

years before Jesus was born, God promised through Isaiah that Jesus would be assigned a grave "with a rich man in his death."[a] This was incredibly unlikely because Jesus was a very poor man who could not have afforded an expensive burial plot. Following Jesus' death, a wealthy and well-known man named Joseph of Arimathea gifted his expensive tomb for the burial of Jesus.[b] As a result, the place of Jesus' burial was easy to confirm. Joseph, who owned the tomb, governmental leaders and their soldiers who were assigned to guard the tomb, and the disciples and women who visited the tomb and found it empty all knew exactly where Jesus' dead body was laid to rest. Had Jesus truly not risen from death, it would have been very easy to prove it by opening the tomb and presenting Jesus' dead body as evidence.

5. *Jesus appeared physically, not just spiritually, alive three days after His death.* Following Jesus' Resurrection, many people touched His physical body: His disciples clung to His feet[c], Mary clung to Him[d], and Thomas the doubter put his hand into the open spear hole in Jesus' side[e]. Jesus also appeared to His disciples after His Resurrection, but they were uncertain if He had truly physically risen from death. Still, Jesus was emphatic about His bodily Resurrection and went out of His way to prove it:

> As they were talking about these things, Jesus himself stood among them, and said to them, "Peace to you!" But they were startled and frightened and thought they saw a spirit. And he said to them, "Why are you troubled, and why do doubts arise in your hearts? See my hands and my feet, that it is I myself. Touch me, and see. For a spirit does not have flesh and bones as you see that I have." And when he had said this, he showed them his hands and his feet. And while they still disbelieved for joy and were marveling, he said to them, "Have you anything here to eat?" They gave him a piece of broiled fish, and he

---

[a] Matt. 27:57-60 [b] Matt. 27:57-60 [c] Matt. 28:9 [d] John 20:17 [e] John 20:20-28

took it and ate before them.[a]

Furthermore, Jesus appeared physically alive over the course of 40 days[b] to crowds as large as 500 people at a time[c]. It is also significant to note that no credible historical evidence from that period exists to validate any alternative explanation for Jesus' Resurrection, other than His literal bodily Resurrection.[123]

6. *Jesus' resurrected body was the same as His pre-Resurrection body.* His disciples recognized Him as the same person who had been crucified[d], and Mary Magdalene recognized Him by the sound of His voice.[e] While Jesus' resurrection body was the same, it was transformed. This explains why Jesus was not always immediately recognized after His Resurrection[f] and seemed to appear and reappear mysteriously.[g] As a Bible scholar noted, "[In] the narratives... it is implied that there was something strange—something unfamiliar or mysterious—in His aspect, which prevented His immediate recognition...which held them in awe."[124] Paul explains this phenomenon in the lengthiest treatment of the nature of a resurrection body in all of Scripture[h]: "It is sown a natural body; it is raised a spiritual body. If there is a natural body, there is also a spiritual body."[i] This "spiritual body" refers to a resurrected body that has been perfected to its glorious state by the power of the Holy Spirit.

7. *Jesus' Resurrection was recorded as Scripture shortly after it occurred.* Mark's Gospel account of the days leading up to Jesus' crucifixion mentions the high priest without naming him.[j] It can logically be inferred that Mark did not mention the high priest by name because he expected his readers to know who he was speaking of. Since Caiaphas was high priest from A.D. 18–37, the latest possible date for the tradition is A.D. 37.[125] This date is so close to the death of Jesus that

---

[a] Luke 24:36-43 [b] Acts 1:3 [c] 1 Cor. 15:6 [d] Luke 24:31; cf. John 21:7,12 [e] John 20:16 [f] John 20:14, 15; 21:4; Luke 24:15-16 [g] John 20:19; Luke 24:31,36 [h] 1 Corinthians 15 [i] 1 Cor. 15:44 [j] Mark 14:53, 54, 60, 61, 63

there would not have been sufficient time for a "legend" of His Resurrection to have developed. This proves that the biblical record of Jesus' Resurrection was penned while the eyewitnesses were still alive to verify the facts. Thus, His Resurrection is not a mythical legend that developed long after the time of Jesus. In fact, one noted scholar who was an academic dean says, "This is the sort of data that historians of antiquity drool over."[126]

8. *Jesus' Resurrection was celebrated in the earliest church creeds.* In 1 Corinthians 15:3-4, Paul says, "…Christ died for our sins in accordance with the Scriptures, that he was buried, that he was raised on the third day in accordance with the Scriptures." This statement is widely accepted as the earliest church creed, which began circulating as early as A.D. 30-36, shortly after Jesus' Resurrection. Considering the early age of this creed, there was not sufficient time between the crucifixion and the creed for any legend about Jesus' Resurrection to accrue. In addition, the witnesses mentioned were still alive and available to be questioned about the facts surrounding the Resurrection.

9. *Jesus' Resurrection convinced His family to worship Him as God.* James, Jesus' half-brother, was originally opposed to the claims of deity by his brother.[a] A transformation occurred in James after seeing his brother resurrected from death.[b] James went on to pastor the church in Jerusalem and authored the New Testament epistle bearing his name.[c] He was also actively involved in shaping the early Church and died to proclaim to everyone that Jesus is the one true God.[d] Also, Jesus' mother Mary was part of the early Church that prayed to and worshiped her son as God[e], as was Jesus' half-brother Jude, who wrote a book of the New Testament bearing his name[f]. While it is not impossible to imagine Jesus convincing some people that He was God if He were not, it is impossible to conceive of Jesus convincing His own devout

---

[a] John 7:5 [b] 1 Cor. 15:7 [c] James 1:1 [d] Acts 12:17; 15:12–21; 21:18; Gal. 2:9 [e] Acts 1:14 [f] Acts 1:14; Jude 1

mother and brothers to suffer persecution in this life and risk the torments of Hell in eternal life for worshiping Him as the one true God unless He truly was.

10. *Jesus' Resurrection was confirmed by His most bitter enemies.* Paul was a devout Jewish Pharisee who routinely persecuted and killed Christians.[a] After an encounter with the risen Christ, Paul was converted and became the most dynamic defender and expander of the Church.[b] Had Jesus not truly risen from death, it is absurd to assume that Paul would ever have worshiped Him as God, particularly when Paul rightly believed that worshiping a false god would send one into the eternal flames of Hell. Simply, Paul hated Jesus and would never have changed his religious practice unless Jesus had risen from death to prove him wrong. Furthermore, Paul insisted that Jesus had risen in almost all his letters in the New Testament.

WHAT IS THE CIRCUMSTANTIAL EVIDENCE FOR JESUS' RESURRECTION?

Effects have causes. Jesus' Resurrection is no exception, as is evident by eight effects caused by it. Together, they are compelling circumstantial evidence for Jesus' Resurrection. Further, for those wanting to deny Jesus' Resurrection, the burden of proof remains on them to account for these multiple effects with a reasonable cause. Christian philosopher William Lane Craig explains, "Anyone who denies this explanation is rationally obligated to produce a more plausible cause of Jesus' resurrection and to explain how it happened."[127] He goes on to assert, "The conclusion that God raised Him up is virtually inescapable. Only a sterile, academic skepticism resists this inevitable inference."[128]

1. *Jesus' disciples were transformed.* Prior to the Resurrection, His disciples were timid and fearful, even hiding when Jesus

---

[a] Phil. 3:4-6 [b] Acts 9

appeared to them.[a] Following the Resurrection, however, they were all transformed into bold witnesses to what they had seen and heard, even to the point of dying in shame and poverty for their convictions, including Peter, their leader, who was crucified upside down rather than denying Christ.

Simon Greenleaf, professor of law at Harvard University and a world-renowned scholar on the rules of legal evidence, said that it was "impossible that they could have persisted in affirming the truths they have narrated, had not Jesus actually risen from the dead, and had they not known this fact as certainly as they knew any other fact."[129]

2. *Jesus' disciples remained loyal to Him as their victorious Messiah.* Modern-day lesser "messiahs" include, for example, politicians who propose to save and deliver us from a terrible fate. Supporters flock around their messiah in hopes that they will deliver on their promise of deliverance. However, when a messiah fails to deliver, their followers either abandon both the cause and the messiah, or they retain the cause and abandon the messiah to instead pursue another messiah. Either way, a failed messiah is a forgotten messiah.

However, Jesus' disciples did not abandon their cause of forgiven sin and life with God or their devotion to Jesus as their victorious Messiah. Furthermore, their devotion to both their cause and Messiah grew in numbers and passionate devotion. They endured widespread persecution and even martyrdom, which would have been unthinkable had Jesus merely died and failed to rise as He promised He would. On this point, historian Kenneth Scott Latourette said:

> It was the conviction of the resurrection of Jesus which lifted his followers out of the despair into which his death had cast them and which led to the perpetuation of the movement begun by him. But for their profound belief that the crucified had risen from the dead and that they had seen him and talked with him, the death of

---
[a] John 20:19

Jesus and even Jesus himself would probably have been all but forgotten.[130]

3. *The disciples had exemplary character.* To claim that the disciples preached obvious lies and deluded people into dying for the world's greatest farce, one would have to first find credible evidence to challenge the character of the disciples. These men were devout Jews who knew that if they worshiped a false god and encouraged others to do the same, they would be sentenced by God to the fires of eternal Hell for violating the first two commandments. Lastly, does not such egregious lying conflict with the character of men and women who gave their lives to feeding the poor, caring for widows and orphans, and helping the hurting and needy?

4. *Worship changed.* The early church stopped worshiping on Saturday, as Jews had for thousands of years, and suddenly began worshiping on Sunday in memory of Jesus' Sunday Resurrection.[a] The Sabbath was so sacred to the Jews that they would not have ceased to obey one of the Ten Commandments unless Jesus had resurrected in fulfillment of their Old Testament Scriptures. Yet, by the end of the first century, Sunday was called "the Lord's Day."[b]

   Not only did the day of worship change after the Resurrection of Jesus, but so did the object of worship. The Ten Commandments forbids the worship of false gods. It is impossible to conceive of devout Jews simply worshiping Jesus as the one true God without the proof of Jesus' Resurrection.

   According to even non-Christian historians, multitudes began worshiping Jesus as the one true God after His Resurrection. Lucian of Samosata was a non-Christian Assyrian-Roman satirist who, around A.D. 170, wrote in mockery of Christians:

   The Christians, you know, worship a man to this day—

---

[a] Acts 20:7; 1 Cor. 16:1-2 [b] Rev. 1:10

the distinguished personage who introduced their novel
rites, and was crucified on that account...You see, these
misguided creatures start with the general conviction that
they are immortal for all time, which explains their
contempt of death and voluntary self-devotion which are
so common among them; and then it was impressed on
them by their original lawgiver that they are all brothers,
from the moment that they are converted, and deny the
gods of Greece, and worship the crucified sage, and live
after his laws.[131]

Additionally, the early Church rejected the observances
of the law because they saw it as having been fulfilled in
Jesus; thus, the law was no longer binding upon them in
the same way as it had been for some 1500 years since Sinai.
This was a cataclysmic shift in belief that was only
considered possible because a new epoch had been ushered in
by the Resurrection of Jesus.

Lastly, God's people welcomed the sacraments of baptism
and communion into their worship of Jesus as God. In
baptism, they remembered Jesus' Resurrection in their
place for their salvation and anticipated their personal future
resurrection. In communion, the early Christians
remembered Jesus' death in their place for their sins.

5. *Women discovered the empty tomb, and they were named* (e.g.
Joanna, Mary Magdalene, Mary Jesus' mother, Mary
mother of James and Joseph, Mary the wife of Clopas, and
Salome). These women were well-known in the early Church
and could have easily been questioned to verify their report.[a]
Moreover, since the testimony of women was not respected in
that culture, it would have been more likely for men to
report discovering the empty tomb if the account was
fictitious. So, the fact that women were the first to arrive at
Jesus' empty tomb proves Scripture is true.

----
[a] Mark 15:40, 47; 16:1

6. *The entirety of early Church preaching centered on the historical fact of Jesus' Resurrection.* If the empty tomb were not a widely accepted fact, the disciples would have reasoned with the skeptics of their day to defend the central issue of their faith. Instead, we see the debate occurring not about whether the tomb was empty, but why it was empty.[132] Furthermore, a reading of the book of Acts shows that, on virtually every occasion that preaching and teaching occurred, the Resurrection of Jesus from death was the central truth being communicated because it had changed human history and could not be ignored. Jesus' Resurrection appears in 12 of the 28 chapters in Acts, which records the history of the early Church.

7. *Jesus' tomb was not enshrined.* Philosopher William Lane Craig says,

> It was customary in Judaism for the tomb of a prophet or holy man to be preserved or venerated as a shrine. This was so because the bones of the prophet lay in the tomb and imparted to the site its religious values. If the remains were not there, then the grave would lose its significance as a shrine.[133]

Of the four major world religions based upon a founder as opposed to a system of ideas, only Christianity claims that the tomb of its founder is empty. Judaism looks back to Abraham, who died almost 4,000 years ago, and still cares for his grave as a holy site at Hebron. Thousands visit Buddha's tomb in India every year. Millions visit the tomb of Mohammed, the founder of Islam, in Medina every year since his death on June 8, A.D. 632.

Additionally, scholar Edwin Yamauchi has discovered evidence that the tombs of at least 50 prophets or other religious figures were enshrined as places of worship and veneration in Palestine around the same time as Jesus' death.[134] Yet, according to one noted scholar, there is "absolutely no trace" of any veneration at Jesus' tomb.[135] The obvious reason for this lack of veneration is that Jesus was not buried but instead resurrected.

8. *Christianity exploded on the earth, and a few billion people today claim to be Christians.* On the same day, in the same place, and in the same way, two other men died, one on Jesus' left and one on His right. Despite the similarities, we do not know the names of these men, and billions of people do not worship them as God. Why? Because they remained dead and Jesus alone rose from death and ascended into Heaven, leaving the Christian church in His wake. On this point, C.F.D. Moule, who held the oldest chair at Cambridge University for 25 years, says, "The birth and rapid rise of the Christian Church...remain an unsolved enigma for any historian who refuses to take seriously the only explanation offered by the Church itself."[136]

WHAT IS THE HISTORICAL EVIDENCE FOR JESUS' RESURRECTION?

Because Jesus' death is a historical fact, the corroborating evidence of non-Christian sources, in addition to the Bible, helps to confirm the Resurrection of Jesus Christ. The following ancient testimony of Romans, Greeks, and Jews is helpful because these men are simply telling the facts without any religious devotion to them.

Josephus (A.D. 37–100)

Josephus was a Jewish historian born just a few years after Jesus. His most celebrated passage, called the "Testimonium Flavianum," says:

> Now there was about this time Jesus, a wise man, if it be lawful to call him a man; for he was a doer of wonderful works, a teacher of such men as receive the truth with pleasure. He drew over to him both many of the Jews and many of the Gentiles. He was [the] Christ. And when

Pilate, at the suggestion of the principal men among us, had condemned him to the cross, those that loved him at the first did not forsake him; for he appeared to them alive again the third day, as the divine prophets had foretold these and ten thousand other wonderful things concerning him. And the tribe of Christians, so named from him, are not extinct at this day.[137]

Suetonius (A.D. 70–160)

Suetonius was a Roman historian and annalist of the Imperial House. In his biography of Nero (who ruled A.D. 54–68), Suetonius mentions the persecution of Christians by indirectly referring to the Resurrection: "Punishment was inflicted on the Christians, a class of men given to a new and mischievous superstition [the resurrection]."[138]

Pliny the Younger (A.D. 61 or 62–113)

Pliny the Younger wrote a letter to the emperor Trajan around A.D. 111 describing early Christian worship gatherings that met early on Sunday mornings in memory of Jesus' Resurrection day:

I have never been present at an examination of Christians. Consequently, I do not know the nature of the extent of the punishments usually meted out to them, nor the grounds for starting an investigation and how far it should be pressed... They also declared that the sum total of their guilt or error amounted to no more than this: they had met regularly before dawn on a fixed day [Sunday in remembrance of Jesus' resurrection] to chant verses alternately amongst themselves in honor of Christ as if to a god.[139]

The Jewish Explanation

The earliest attempt to provide an alternative explanation

for the Resurrection of Jesus did not deny that the tomb was empty.[a] Instead, opponents claimed that the body had been stolen, thus admitting the fact of the empty tomb. But this explanation is untenable for the following reasons. (1) The tomb was closed with an enormous rock and sealed by the government, and there is no explanation for how the rock was moved while being guarded by armed Roman soldiers. (2) If the body had been stolen, a large ransom could have been offered to the thieves, and they could have been coerced to produce the body. Or if it had been taken by the disciples, then the torture and death they suffered should have been sufficient to return the body. (3) Even if the body was stolen, how are we to account for the fact that Jesus appeared to multiple crowds of people, proving that He was alive? In conclusion, the theft of the body is unlikely and still fails to account for it returning back to life.

Summarily, the historical testimony of those who were not Christians stands in agreement with Scripture that Jesus died and rose because those are the historical facts. Thomas Arnold, former professor of modern history at Oxford, said, "No one fact in the history of mankind . . . is proved by better and fuller evidence of every sort" than the fact that "Christ died and rose from the dead."[140]

WHAT ARE THE PRIMARY ANCIENT OBJECTIONS TO JESUS' RESURRECTION?

The Resurrection of Jesus Christ is the fact upon which Christianity is founded. Simply stated, if Jesus is dead, then Christianity is the greatest lie ever told, and the Christian Church is guilty of the greatest deception ever. William Lyon Phelps (distinguished professor at Yale for 40 years) said,

In the whole story of Jesus Christ, the most important event is the resurrection. Christian faith depends on this. It is encouraging to know that it is explicitly given by

––––––––––
[a] Matt. 28:13-15

all four evangelists and told also by Paul. The names of those who saw Him after His triumph over death are recorded; and it may be said that the historical evidence for the resurrection is stronger than for any other miracle anywhere narrated; for as Paul said, if Christ is not risen from the dead then is our preaching in vain, and your faith is also vain.[141]

To defend the fact upon which Christianity stands or falls, we will now examine the primary objections to Jesus' Resurrection to see if any are credible.

Jesus did not die on the cross but merely swooned.

Some have argued that Jesus did not in fact die on the cross but rather swooned or basically passed out and therefore appeared dead. Regarding this claim, Bible teacher John Stott has asked if we are to believe that after the rigors and pains of trial, mockery, flogging, and crucifixion. He could survive 36 hours in a stone sepulcher with neither warmth nor food nor medical care. Are we to believe that He could then rally sufficiently to perform the superhuman feat of shifting the boulder which secured the mouth of the tomb, and this without disturbing the Roman guard? That then, weak and sickly and hungry, He could appear to the disciples in such a way as to give them the impression that He had vanquished death? That He could go on to claim that He had died and risen, could send them into all the world and promise to be with them unto the end of time? That He could live somewhere in hiding for 40 days, making occasional surprise appearances, and then finally disappear without explanations? Such credulity is more incredible than Thomas' unbelief.[142]

Crucifixion is essentially death by asphyxiation because the prisoner grows too tired to lift himself up and fill his lungs with air. This explains why the Romans would often break a prisoner's legs, thus preventing him from continuing to fill his lungs with air. Since the professional executioners did not break Jesus' legs, these professional executioners must have been convinced of His death.[a] Jesus' only chance of deceiving the executioners was to stop breathing, which would have killed Him.

Lastly, John 19:34–35 tells us that the Roman soldier thrust a spear into Jesus' heart to confirm His death. The water that poured out was probably from the sac surrounding His heart, and the blood most likely came from the right side of His heart. Even if He had been alive, this would have killed Him.[143]

Jesus did not rise, and His body was stolen.

The original explanation given for the empty tomb by those who did not choose to worship Jesus as God was that the tomb was indeed empty, not because of a resurrection but because of a theft of Jesus' dead body.[b] For this to be true, a number of impossibilities would have had to occur. (1) Despite the fact that it would have cost them their lives, all the guards positioned at the tomb would have had to fall asleep at the same time. (2) Each of the guards would have had to not only fall asleep but also remain asleep and not be awakened by the breaking of the Roman seal on the tomb, the rolling away of the enormous stone which blocked the entrance, or the carrying off of the dead body. (3) Even if Jesus' body was stolen, there is no way to account for its returning to vibrant and triumphant life. The issue of motive is also a key factor in refuting this hypothesis. What benefit would there be for the disciples to risk their lives to steal a corpse and die for a lie as a result? What motive would there be for the Jews, Romans, or anyone else to steal the body? And if the body were truly stolen, could not a bounty have been offered and someone enticed to provide it in exchange for a handsome cash reward?

A twin brother, or a look-alike, died in Jesus' place.

It has been suggested that Jesus was not the one crucified but rather a brother or other man who looked like Him.

---

[a] John 19:31-33 [b] Matt. 28:11-15

However, there is not a shred of evidence to prove that someone who looked like Jesus existed at that time. Additionally, Jesus' mother was present at His crucifixion, and the likelihood of fooling His mother is minimal. Also, the physical wounds He suffered during the crucifixion were visible on Jesus' resurrection body and carefully inspected by the disciple Thomas, who was very doubtful that Jesus had risen until he touched scars from the crucifixion evident on Jesus' body.[a] In addition, the tomb was empty, and the burial cloths were left behind.

Jesus' followers hallucinated His Resurrection.

Some people have suggested that the disciples did not actually see Jesus risen from death but rather hallucinated, or projected, their desires for His Resurrection into a hallucination. John Dominic Crossan, co-chairman of the Jesus Seminar, told *Time Magazine* that after the crucifixion, Jesus' corpse was probably laid in a shallow grave, barely covered with dirt, and eaten by wild dogs. The subsequent story of Jesus' Resurrection, he says, was merely the result of "wishful thinking."[144]

This thesis is unbelievable for five reasons. (1) A hallucination is a private, not public, experience. Yet Jesus appeared to more than 500 people at one time.[b] (2) Jesus appeared in a variety of times at a variety of locations, whereas hallucinations are generally restricted to individual times and places. (3) Certain types of people tend to be more prone to hallucination than others. Yet Jesus appeared to a great variety of personalities, including His brothers and mother. (4) After 40 days, Jesus' appearances suddenly stopped for everyone simultaneously. Hallucinations tend to continue over longer periods of time and do not stop abruptly. (5) A hallucination is a projection of a thought that preexists in the mind. However, the Jews had a conception of resurrection that applied to the raising of all people at the end of history[c], not the raising of any

---

[a] John 20:24-28 [b] 1 Cor. 15:1–6 [c] E.g., Dan. 12:2

particular individual in the middle of history.[145] Therefore, it is inconceivable that the witnesses to the Resurrection could have hallucinated Jesus' Resurrection.

Jesus rose from death spiritually, but not physically.

One Bible scholar says,

Jehovah's Witnesses believe that when Jesus Christ was alive in the flesh He was simply and solely a human being—no more, and no less. From the first Russell [a founder Charles Taze Russell] had dismissed the idea of two natures in the one Christ. Jesus was not "a combination of two natures, human and spiritual" for such a "blending" would produce "neither the one nor the other, but an imperfect hybrid thing, which is obnoxious to the divine arrangement." That being so, "when Jesus was in the flesh, he was a perfect human being; previous to that time, he was a perfect spiritual being; and since his resurrection he is a perfect spiritual being."[146]

Jesus denied this view. In Luke 24:36–40, following His Resurrection, Jesus

stood among them, and said to them, "Peace to you!" But they were startled and frightened and thought they saw a spirit [or angel]. And he said to them . . . "See my hands and my feet, that it is I myself. Touch me, and see. For a spirit does not have flesh and bones as you see that I have." And when he had said this, he showed them his hands and his feet.

Then Jesus had breakfast, hugged His friends, and showed doubters the scars in His hands and side, which are things that an angelic being without a physical body cannot do.

WHAT HAS THE RESURRECTION ACCOMPLISHED FOR CHRISTIANS?

Those who come into God's family will be joined to Jesus in His death and resurrection life.[a] Regarding our future, Jesus' Resurrection is the precedent and pattern of our own: "Christ has been raised from the dead, the firstfruits of those who have fallen asleep."[b] As His body was resurrected in complete health, so too will we rise and never experience pain, injury, or death ever again. Through the Resurrection, Jesus has put death to death. Because Jesus rose from death physically, we learn that God, through Christ, intends to reclaim and restore all that He made in creation and saw corrupted through the sinful Fall. Our eternity will be spent in a world much like the one enjoyed by our first parents in Eden because the earth has been reclaimed and restored by God through Jesus' Resurrection. If you belong to Jesus Christ, you need not fear death and can look past your grave, in faith, that Jesus has eternal resurrection life for you along with all other believers! This completely transforms how we live and how we die because Jesus changes everything!

---

[a] Romans 6:3-5 [b] 1 Cor. 15:20

CHAPTER 9

IS KING JESUS THE ONLY WAY TO HEAVEN?

Jesus said to him, "I am the way, and the truth, and the life. No one comes to the Father except through me..." – John 14:6

One thing that every generation and culture holds in common is a hopeful longing for a savior. Living in our fallen, broken, cursed world causes us to long for more. Because God made us for perfection, we cannot simply accept life under the curse and long for someone to come and deliver us as our savior.

In ancient Greek culture, philosophers like Epicurus, gods like Zeus, and rulers like Ptolemy were heralded as saviors. Likewise, in ancient Roman culture, the emperors from Nero's family line were also considered saviors.

In every election, candidates are presented as nothing short of saviors. Joining them are CEOs of companies who are hired as saviors who will snatch a company and its investors from a fiery Hell of decreased profits. Any sports fan will tell you that there is a player that, if their team could just sign them, would save the season and guarantee victory. Additionally, it seems like every pharmaceutical commercial on television touts yet another pill as some sort of savior to make life in a cursed world sheer bliss.

The human desire for a divine human savior is seemingly insatiable. This explains why we invent comic book heroes who are, in many ways, both human and divine knockoffs of Christ, and we deify our heroes like Martin Luther King Jr. and John F. Kennedy, who were both well-known philanderers, not sinless like Jesus. This desire for human saviors also explains why little boys always want to be saviors when they grow up, so they dress up like firemen, soldiers, police officers, Batman, Spiderman, Superman, or Wolverine.

Religions also have their own concepts of a savior. In Buddhism, you save yourself by ceasing all desire. In Confucianism, you save yourself through education, self-reflection, self-cultivation, and living a moral life. In Hinduism, you save yourself by detaching yourself from the separated ego and trying to live in unity with the divine. In Islam, you save yourself by living a life of good deeds. In Orthodox Judaism, you save yourself through repentance, prayer, and working hard to obey the Law. In New Ageism, you save yourself by gaining a new perspective, through which you see how you are connected to all things as a divine oneness. In Taoism, you save yourself by aligning yourself with the Tao to have peace and harmony in and around you. What nearly all religions and spiritualities hold in common is the theme that if there is a savior, it is the people saving themselves.

GOD ALONE IS OUR SAVIOR

The concept of God alone being our savior and therefore the only source of our hope is a common theme throughout the Old Testament, especially in the books of Psalms and Isaiah. Isaiah 43:11 says, "I, I am the Lord, and besides me there is no savior." Isaiah 45:21 says, "…there is no other god besides me, a righteous God and a Savior; there is none besides me." Isaiah 62:11 says, "Behold, the Lord has proclaimed to the end of the earth: Say to the daughter of Zion, 'Behold, your salvation comes; behold, his reward is with him, and his recompense before him.'" In summary, God Himself says that there is no savior apart from Him, no savior like Him, and that He alone is the savior for all the nations of the earth. Furthermore, our Savior God was promised to come into human history to gift salvation to us. From the days of Isaiah forward, God's people were then awaiting the coming of that savior, Jesus Christ.

JESUS IS OUR SAVIOR GOD

The word "savior" appears 24 times in the New Testament, with eight occurrences referring to God in general and 16 referring to Jesus in particular. Titus 2:13 speaks of "our great God and Savior Jesus Christ…"

In addition to the word savior, related words such as "save" and "salvation" also appear frequently throughout the New Testament. They, too, point to Jesus as our God and Savior, including an angel declaring that Jesus would be born to "save his people from their sins."[a] In this instance, God Himself announces the coming of Jesus through an angel as the fulfillment of the promises given through Isaiah hundreds of years prior. Furthermore, it was commanded by God that the boy born to the Virgin Mary be named "Jesus," which means God saves His people from their sins.

At the birth of Jesus, an angel also declared that "a Savior" had been born.[b] Upon seeing the newborn Jesus, the godly old man Simeon, held the baby Jesus in his arms and said, "...my eyes have seen your salvation."[c] Therefore, God promised in the Old Testament that Jesus was coming as our savior, announced His imminent arrival through the womb of Mary, and then declared His arrival at the birth of Jesus.

JESUS SAVES MANY PEOPLE

Not only is Jesus our Savior, but He is also a global savior, saving people from every generation, nation, race, culture, tribe, and tongue. Many religions have a false concept of a savior who is only concerned with their people group and disinterested or even opposed to people from other races, nations, and cultures.

Scripture speaks of Jesus as the savior of the Jews.[d] Jesus came into history as a Jew, lived his life as a Jew, and was seen by many Jews as the fulfillment of the Old Testament promises about the coming of a savior. As a result, much of the early church was comprised of Jews.

Jesus is also the savior of the Church.[e] This means that while there are expressions of the global Church in various local churches, denominations, and networks, Jesus is, in fact, the savior of all Christians who would come to Him in repentant faith.

Jesus is the savior of the world.[f] Revelation 5:9 paints Jesus as the global, multicultural savior: "...by your blood you ransomed people for God from every tribe and language and people and nation..."

---

[a] Matt 1:21 [b] Luke 2:11 [c] Luke 2:28-30 [d] Acts 5:30-31 [e] Eph 5:23 [f] 1 John 4:14

Jesus is the savior of the lost.[a] In this way, Jesus is utterly unlike the view of a savior offered by religion. Religion says that we have gotten ourselves lost and we need to follow the path laid out for us by religion and rediscover our way home. Unlike religion, Jesus knows that we are hopelessly lost, and without His coming to seek us and save us, we are forever doomed.

Lastly, Jesus is the savior of sinners like us. The man who perhaps most clearly understood this was Paul, who had gone from a murderer of Christians to a Christian pastor. If ever there was a man who was unfit for God to save, it was Paul. By saving Paul, Jesus demonstrated what a glorious savior he is. Paul wrote,

> The saying is trustworthy and deserving of full acceptance, that Christ Jesus came into the world to save sinners, of whom I am the foremost. But I received mercy for this reason, that in me, as the foremost, Jesus Christ might display his perfect patience as an example to those who were to believe in him for eternal life. To the King of ages, immortal, invisible, the only God, be honor and glory forever and ever. Amen.[b]

One of the wonderful encouragements of Jesus being our savior is that God can and will save even the guiltiest of wretched sinners who turn to Jesus in repentant faith. No one, and nothing, is beyond His saving hand: "everyone who calls on the name of the Lord will be saved."[c]

Without Jesus' salvation by grace alone, all we are left with is the pathetic false god of religion that only loves the good guys and not the bad guys, offering no hope for sinners. The hard truth is that we are all sinners. As a result, we cannot save ourselves but need our sinless Savior to do our saving.

---

[a] Luke 19:10 [b] 1 Tim 1:15-17 [c] Rom. 10:13

JESUS SAVES PEOPLE FROM MANY THINGS

While there is only one savior, He saves us from many things. For the sake of brevity, we will mention only four.

Jesus saves us from sin.[a] Rather than accepting or hiding our sin, we can put sin to death and live new lives with Jesus.

Jesus saves us from death.[b] Because death is the penalty and consequence of sin, Jesus' death was, as the Puritan John Owen said, "the death of death." Our greatest enemy, death, no longer rules over God's children because Jesus has saved them from death.

Jesus saves us from Satan.[c] Because of our sin, we are captive to Satan. But Jesus' authority has been delegated to His people so that they can live in victory over Satan and demons.

Jesus saves us from God's wrath and Hell.[d] To be a Christian is to be a guilty person saved from God's holy and just wrath.[e] The crucifixion of Jesus was a precursor of the eternity awaiting the unrepentant in Hell and a compelling reason for us to turn to Jesus so that we might be saved from the penalty for our sin. While some people struggle with the idea of a loving God sending people to Hell, what is more perplexing is how a holy God could allow anyone into Heaven! Through the work of Jesus our savior, who endured the wrath of God in our place for our sins, we can and will be saved.

An honest Christian will tell you that Jesus also saved them from themselves. If you are a Christian, in all honesty, who would you be, and what would you be doing if Jesus had not saved you from yourself? I am certain that, without Jesus Christ, there is zero percent chance I would be a pastor enjoying teaching the Bible and leading His people, and next to a zero percent chance I would be faithfully married to my wife as we have been since August 15, 1992, and have a loving, close, joyful relationship with all our kids and grandkids. Without Jesus, I would have made our life hell and then died to go to Hell.

----

[a] Matt 1:21 [b] 2 Tim 1:10 [c] 2 Thess 2:6-10 [d] Rom 5:9 [e] Rom 5:9-10

JESUS IS OUR ONLY SAVIOR

In our day of tolerance and diversity, it is perhaps most controversial to state that Jesus is the only savior, which makes Him distinct from and superior to any other proposed savior. The Buddha taught that there are 84,000 paths to enlightenment, which makes as much sense as saying 84,000 different roads going in different directions all lead to the same destination. Mahatma Gandhi wrongly said, "Religions are different roads converging to the same point."[147]

Are we to believe that the atheist road (which says there is no God), the agnostic road (which is unsure if there is a God), and the Hindu road (which says there are millions of gods) all lead to the same place? Are we to believe that the road that says there is no life after death, the road that says you reincarnate, and the road that says you stand before Jesus for judgment and sentencing to eternal Heaven or Hell all lead to the same place? Are we truly to believe that the road that says we save ourselves leads to the same place as the road that says only Jesus can save us?

The exclusivity, superiority, and singularity of Jesus are precisely the teaching of Scripture. This anchoring truth, that Jesus is our only savior, is in many ways responsible for much of the opposition and persecution that Christians from the early church to the present have encountered. Peter, filled and led by God the Holy Spirit, proclaimed with all certainty in Acts 4:12, "…there is salvation in no one else, for there is no other name under heaven given among men by which we must be saved." Indeed, when we are speaking of salvation, we must speak only of Jesus, always of Jesus, and assuredly of Jesus.

Christianity is not alone in saying its beliefs supplant all others. Every faith and every belief system make exclusive claims. In fact, anyone who asserts anything proves they implicitly accept some things as true and reject others as false. It doesn't matter whether the subject of conversation is Christ or college basketball or climate change.

From our standpoint as Christians, a world full of religious options boils down to two things: good works or God's grace. It is one or the other. Other religions require good works—living a moral life, obeying the law, reincarnating to pay off your karmic debt, etc. Christianity holds to God's grace—getting to Heaven not because of what we do but because of what Jesus has done. We do not ascend to God through our piety or good works. God became man to reconcile mankind to God. Like the apostle Paul wrote, "For, There is one God and one Mediator who can reconcile God and humanity—the man Christ Jesus. He gave his life to purchase freedom for everyone. This is the message God gave to the world at just the right time."[a] What we believe *is* different.

The exclusivism of the Christian faith is more than a theoretical abstraction. It gets to the core of how we relate to God. The Bible repeatedly says that God loves His people like a husband loves His wife. We might consider His exclusive demands intolerant, bigoted, and close-minded, but they actually reflect His relentless pursuit of a loving, unique, and devoted relationship. When the God of the Bible sees people chasing other gods, He feels like a husband who walks in on his wife with another man. When they dabble in other religions and spiritualties, God calls it adultery.[b]

ONE LOVING WAY

All the exclusive claims of Jesus need to be heard in that context of God's relentless love. When Jesus speaks truth about who He is and what He has done, His words flow from nothing less than His infinite love.

It is not mean for a Christian to tell others that Jesus alone saves. It is like warning a friend getting sucked into a bad relationship. You see danger, but they have been duped. Speaking up might feel uncomfortable, but it is the only compassionate choice.

Illusionist and atheist Penn Jillette talks about getting handed a Bible after a show. "I wanted you to have this," the man said. "I'm kind of proselytizing. I'm a businessman. I'm

---

[a] 1 Tim. 2:5–6, NLT [b] Jeremiah 3:1-5 and the entire book of Hosea illustrate this point

sane. I'm not crazy." The man likely knew he was talking to a resolute atheist, but he was neither aggressive nor defensive. He just looked Jillette in the eye, said some kind words about the show, and gave his gift. The outspoken Jillette says this about the encounter:

> I don't respect people who don't proselytize. I don't respect that at all. If you believe that there's a heaven and hell, and people could be going to hell—or not getting eternal life or whatever—and you think that, well, it's not really worth telling them this because it would make it socially awkward…How much do you have to hate somebody not to proselytize? How much do you have to hate somebody to believe that everlasting life is possible and not tell them that?

Jillette concludes, "This guy was a really good guy. Polite and honest and sane—and he cared enough about me to proselytize and give me a Bible."[148]

THE NARROW DOOR

Many Bible passages clarify the exclusive, all-important claims of Jesus regarding salvation. One of the most obvious is Luke 13:22–30. Someone asked Jesus a question for the ages: "Lord, will those who are saved be few?" Jesus' reply is what we will now study.

Salvation is one narrow door.
"Strive to enter through the narrow door," Jesus responded. "For many, I tell you, will seek to enter and will not be able…"[a] Every home has a door, and God's heavenly home is no exception. The door separates insiders from outsiders, family from foe, and those who are welcome from those not on the guest list. God lives on one side, and we live on the other. On His side is holiness, and on our side sin. And the door between

----
[a] Luke 13:24

us and God is "narrow." What does that mean? Few find the door. Fewer still go through it. Apart from this door, there is no salvation, no forgiveness of sin, no hope for sinners, and no eternal life. The only door of salvation is narrow indeed.

The narrow door is exclusive and inclusive.
Christianity is the most exclusive of all religions because there is only one door. But it is also the most inclusive because *all* are welcome to pass through the one narrow door. In some religions, you must be of a particular race, ethnicity, or people group, but not so in Christianity. All nations are invited to pass through the narrow door of salvation. In some religions, you need to learn Hebrew or Arabic, but all languages can enter here. In some religions, you must be smart and studious, but at the narrow door even the simple can find the way in. In some religions, you need to be rich so you can buy your seat or go through layers of teaching, training, and cleansing, but at this door, the poorest of the poor are welcomed.

The narrow door is closing.
God has opened a door of invitation. But that door will close. Jesus said, "When once the master of the house has risen and shut the door, and you begin to stand outside and to knock at the door, saying, 'Lord, open to us,' then he will answer you, 'I do not know where you come from.'"[a] There is no reincarnation, no annihilation, and no second chance for salvation after death. You live, you die, you are judged. That is the truth. When you die, the door of salvation slams shut behind you.

The narrow door divides Heaven and Hell.
Jesus says this narrow door divides Heaven and Hell. He first describes Hell: "In that place there will be weeping and gnashing of teeth, when you see...the kingdom of God but you yourselves cast out." And then Jesus describes Heaven: "And people will come...and recline at table in the kingdom of

---
[a] Luke 13:25

180

God…"[a] Hell lasts just as long as Heaven: forever.

The narrow door IS Jesus.
In the end, Jesus reveals that He is that narrow door. His death opens the way for us to enter Heaven. God has opened one narrow door from us to Him, and that door is Jesus Christ, who says, "I am the door. If anyone enters by me, he will be saved…"[b] Jesus died in our place for our sins as our substitute and Savior and rose to open Heaven. Jesus says, "I am the door!" He is the door of salvation, the door of invitation, the door from man to God, and the door from Hell to Heaven.

For Christians, there is no getting around the fact that Jesus is the door separating salvation and damnation. Atheists are wrong: God is real, and there is a world beyond this world and a life after this life. Pluralists make a grave mistake: There are not multiple doors leading to eternal life, and not all religions go to the same place. And universalists lie: Not everyone dies and goes to Heaven. Simply dying does not usher anyone into paradise. The decision we make in this life for or against Christ ultimately determines where we go at life's end forever and ever. Once we die, the door closes, and the opportunity for salvation is gone forever.

Have you turned from sin and trusted in Jesus Christ as your Savior? If not, it should be of the utmost urgency to you. Forever is a long time, and the wrath of God in Hell is real. We want to see you in Heaven and wrote this entire book to plead with you to receive Jesus and not go to Hell.

---

[a] Luke 13:28-29 [b] John 10:9

CHAPTER 10

WHAT DIFFERENCE HAS KING JESUS MADE IN HISTORY?

"There's nothing we can do. Look, everyone has gone after him!"
–Jesus' critics, frustrated by His popularity (John 12:19, NLT)

No one and no thing is bigger than Jesus Christ. All of human history is covered by the towering shadow of His influence.

When the new millennium was on the horizon, *Newsweek* ran the cover story, "2000 Years of Jesus: Holy Wars to Helping Hands—How Christianity Shaped the Modern World." The article said,

> By any secular standard, Jesus is also the dominant figure of Western culture. Like the millennium itself, much of what we now think of as Western ideas, inventions, and values finds its source or inspiration in the religion that worships God in his name. Art and science, the self and society, politics and economics, marriage and the family, right and wrong, body and soul—all have been touched and often radically transformed by the Christian influence.[149]

The *Newsweek* issue also included a poll in which Americans were asked, "If there had never been a Jesus, do you think there would be more, less, or about the same amount of war, charity, and happiness?"[150] Regarding war, 48 percent of people thought there would be more, 15 percent thought less, and 24 percent thought it would be the same. Regarding charity, 7 percent thought there would be more, 64 percent thought there would be less, and 18 percent thought it would be the same. Regarding happiness, 9 percent thought there would be more, 57 percent thought there would be less, and 20 percent thought there would be the same had Jesus never lived. Even non-Christians agree that Jesus has helped human history.

More books have been written about Jesus than anyone who has ever lived. Numerous chronicle Jesus' effect on history, such as His place in various centuries[151] and His place in pop culture.[152]

English writer H. G. Wells said, "I am an historian, I am not a believer, but I must confess as a historian that this penniless preacher from Nazareth is irrevocably the very center of history. Jesus Christ is easily the most dominant figure in all history."[153]

Historian and Yale Religion Department Chair Kenneth Scott Latourette said, "As the centuries pass, the evidence is accumulating that, measured by His effect on history, Jesus is the most influential life ever lived on this planet." Lastly, an inscription at the entrance to Rockefeller Center, New York City, says, "Man's ultimate destiny depends not on whether he can learn new lessons or make new discoveries and conquests, but on the acceptance of the lesson taught him close upon two thousand years ago."

Jesus looms so largely over history that we measure historical time in the context of His life. B.C. refers to the time "before Christ," and A.D. (*anno Domini*) means "in the year of the Lord." Our biggest holidays are dedicated to Him as we celebrate His birth every Christmas and Resurrection every Easter.

Nations, causes, and leaders have come and gone. But for more than 2,000 years, the Church of Jesus Christ has spread from one nation to the nations, from the language of Hebrew to thousands of languages, and from one generation to generation after generation. Christianity ranks as the most popular religion and the largest and longest-standing movement of any kind in the history of the planet, with more than two billion people today claiming to be followers of Jesus Christ.

While the life of Jesus was simple, the legacy of Jesus is stunning. Jesus is not only worshiped as God by one-third of the people on planet earth, but no army or king has wrought as much influence on history as He. To illustrate this point, we will briefly examine some of the differences Jesus has made in history.

JESUS AND CHILDREN

Tragically, the plight of children in the ancient world was horrendous. Both child sacrifice and child abandonment were common. Only half of all children lived beyond the age of eight. It was not uncommon for people to discard healthy babies by simply placing them out with the trash to be taken by the worst kind of people, who abused the children, sold them into prostitution, or forced them into slavery.

The coming of Jesus made an enormous difference in the treatment of children. Because Jesus Himself had been a child born into poverty to a single mother, He was seen by many children in tragic circumstances as giving them both dignity and hope. By coming as a child, Jesus honored childhood.

Although He Himself did not have any children, Jesus loved and cared for children. Jesus taught that God is a loving Father and that we are His children who should treat our children as our Father treats us.[a] In the Gospel of Matthew alone, Jesus healed children[b], said that God imparts wisdom to children[c], taught children[d], said Heaven was made for children[e], said that God would punish anyone who harmed a child[f], laid His hands on children to pray over them[g], invited children to Himself[h], cast demons out of tormented children[i], and was worshiped by children.[j]

Furthermore, Jesus Himself was born of a single mother and was adopted by the godly man Joseph. Building on this same metaphor, the New Testament teaches that in our salvation, God acts in much the same way; he is our Father who adopts us into his family, the Church.[k] As God's people began seeing themselves as spiritual orphans who had been adopted by God the Father, they not only treated children with great dignity as God's image bearers like Jesus did, but they also began adopting discarded children and telling them about Jesus as a demonstration of the gospel. This practice continues throughout the world today with orphanages, foster care, and adoption, whereby God's people demonstrate the gospel of Jesus Christ to children.

JESUS AND WOMEN

In many ancient and modern cultures, women were and

---

[a] Matt 7:11 [b] Matt 9:23-25 [c] Matt 11:25 [d] Matt 14:21 [e] Matt 18:3; 19:14 [f] Matt 18:5-6 [g] Matt 19:13 [h] Matt 19:14 [i] Matt 17:14-18 [j] Matt 21:15 [k] Rom 8:12-23; Gal 4:1-7; Eph 1:5

still are essentially regarded as the property of their husbands. For example, in India, if a woman's husband died, she could be burned alive on her husband's funeral pyre in a ceremony called suttee. She had no value living apart from her husband. Likewise, infanticide was commonly practiced for girls in India, along with "child widows," or little girls raised to be temple prostitutes, until the coming of Christian missionaries such as William Carey and Amy Carmichael.

Conversely, the Bible teaches that God made us male and female and that men and women, though different, are absolutely equal because they both bear the image of God.[a] Furthermore, while not sinning, Jesus did often violate social taboos regarding women and, in doing so, honored them. Examples include when He befriended the Samaritan woman at the well of Sychar[b] and spoke publicly with the widow of Nain.[c] Jesus often healed and cast demons out of women.[d] Jesus used women as examples of exemplary faith in His teachings.[e] In what was likely quite controversial because women were generally omitted from theological instruction, Jesus did teach women theology.[f] Jesus allowed Himself to be anointed by a sinful woman.[g] Two of Jesus' closest friends were women, whom he loved like sisters.[h] The funding of Jesus' ministry included generous support from godly women.[i] Lastly, the Bible records that godly women were the first to know that Jesus had risen from death.[j] In summary, Jesus honored, taught, and loved women and even included them in vital positions in His ministry.

Historian Rodney Stark says,

In Roman as in Jewish society, women were regarded as inherently inferior to men. Husbands could divorce their wives but wives could not divorce their husbands. In rabbinic circles, only males were allowed to study the Torah. Jesus challenged these arrangements. Although he called only men to be apostles, Jesus readily accepted

---

[a] Gen 1:26-27 [b] John 4:7-26 [c] Luke 7:12-13 [d] Matt 9:20-22; Luke 8:40-56; 13:10-17 [e] Matt 25:1-10; Luke 4:26; 18:1-5; 21:1-4 [f] Luke 10:38-42; 23:27-31; John 20:10-18 [g] Luke 7:36-50 [h] Luke 10:38-39 [i] Luke 8:1-3 [j] Matt 28:1-10

women into his circle of friends and disciples... Christianity's appeal for women was a major reason that it grew so rapidly in competition with other religions of the Roman Empire. Then, as now, most Christians were women. The new religion offered women not only greater status and influence within the church but also more protection as wives and mothers.[154]

JESUS AND SLAVERY AND RACISM

In the days of Jesus, roughly half of the people in the Roman Empire were slaves. By calling Himself a servant or slave, Jesus identified Himself with those who were enslaved. Following Jesus' teaching, Paul listed slave trading as among the most heinous of sins and pleaded for the merciful treatment of a Christian slave named Onesimus.[a]

In an email interview I had with #1 bestselling author Eric Metaxas, he said, "It was Christians who fought passionately to end the slave trade and slavery itself. William Wilberforce and other Christians stood against secularists and for African slaves precisely because they believed that all men are brothers, and all human beings are created in the image of God. Those who did not believe the Bible thought that notion a joke and thought the darker-skinned races to be as obviously inferior to the light-skinned races as dogs were superior to rats or bugs."

Scholar Wayne Grudem added in a personal interview that two-thirds of the leaders of the American abolitionist movement were Christians preaching that slavery should end. In more recent years, it was Christians like Rosa Parks, Jackie Robinson, and Martin Luther King Jr. who used biblical imagery and language to move a nation to stand against racial injustice, as Metaxas pointed out in our interview.

In the United States, the fight against slavery was led in large part by Christians. Their number included President Abraham Lincoln, who is widely regarded as perhaps the most important American to fight against slavery.

------

[a] 1 Timothy 1:8-11; Philemon 10-19

Christians across time and geography have followed Jesus' example of welcoming all peoples. Today, Jesus is worshiped among more races and cultures in more languages than anyone in history. There is simply no organization of any kind that has as much diversity as Christianity because the Bible teaches that we all equally bear God's image.

JESUS AND EDUCATION

As a teacher, Jesus the rabbi has made an unparalleled difference in education. Because Christians are people of the Book, as Christianity has spread, so has language translation, publishing, education, and literacy. In fact, the Bible is the most translated, sold, and read book in world history!

Many of the world's languages were first written down by missionaries seeking to translate the Bible into the native language of a people group. For groups that lack a written language, Christians have often created one for them.

In the so-called Dark Ages, many of the classics of Western literature were preserved by priests and monks who hand-copied them and started the first European universities in cities like Paris and Bologna. The printing press was invented by the Christian Johannes Gutenberg (1398–1468) for the printing of Bibles and other Christian literature. Jesus never wrote a book, but the Library of Congress holds more books about Jesus (17,000) than about any other historical figure, roughly twice as many as Shakespeare, the runner-up.[155] One University of Chicago scholar has estimated that more has been written about Jesus in the last 20 years than in the previous 19 centuries combined.[156]

With the landing of the Christian Puritans in America came literacy and education. From 1620, when the pilgrims landed, until 1837, virtually all American education was private and Christian. In the 19th century colonies of Massachusetts and Connecticut, the literacy rate among men ranged from 89 to 95 percent. The pastors in the colonies were often the most educated men and led both the intellectual and spiritual life of the people. In Puritan New England, the first schools (known as common schools) were founded and were distinctively Christian. Soon, tax monies were raised to support these schools, and the first public schools in the United States were Christian and remained that way for 217 years.

Regarding higher education, nearly every one of the first 123 American colleges and universities founded in the United States was of Christian origins, including Yale, William and Mary, Brown, Princeton, NYU, and Northwestern. Harvard was started by a donation of money and books by Rev. John Harvard. Dartmouth was founded to train missionaries.

The practice of Christian education for all continues in many other nations where Christian schools have been established by missionaries. For example, Nelson Mandela, who has been lauded by many as a hero for his stand against apartheid, graduated from two missionary schools.

JESUS AND AMERICA

America was, as a general rule, founded as an experiment in religious freedom by professing Christians. The inauguration of our first president, George Washington, included him kneeling to kiss the Bible before leading the Senate and House of Representatives to a church for a two-hour worship service. In fact, 34 percent of all the Founding Fathers' citations in books, pamphlets, articles, and other works were from the Bible.[157]

Among the most practical benefits of the Christian influence on our nation's founding are the rule of law, equality of all citizens under the law, rights granted to us by God our Creator, and individual liberty as the foundational principles undergirding our rule of law. Additionally, the Christian belief of human sinfulness helped to create the separation of government into three branches in an effort to avoid unchecked power in the hands of sinners.

JESUS AND SCIENCE

For science to operate, there must first exist a worldview that provides a comprehensive understanding of how the world works and our place in it. Because Christianity teaches that behind creation is a God of order who made us to explore His world, scientific exploration and discovery were possible. Scientific inquiry would not have been possible in other religious worldviews so fatalistic that change is not possible or so animistic that scientific study would be religiously condemned. Various Eastern religions see reality as little more than an illusion that is therefore unable to be scientifically explored. This, in part, explains why Christians such as geneticist Francis Collins (director of the National Human Genome Research Project and a Christian) see no conflict between their faith in Jesus and their work as scientists. Collins, in fact, explains the relationship between his saving faith in the Creator and his scientific exploration of creation in his book *The Language of God: A Scientist Presents Evidence for Belief.*

JESUS AND ECONOMICS

The influence of Jesus and Christianity has also been profound in the world of economics. For brevity, we will mention only two important factors.

The Bible teaches private property rights; the Ten Commandments forbid stealing anyone's private property simply because it rightfully belongs to its owner. This simple principle is one of the pillars on which our entire economy is built. In nations where Christianity has not spread, this principle is not accepted, and, for example, the government owns people's homes and reserves the right to seize their property.

The Bible also teaches that all work is sacred if done for the glory of God. Jesus Himself modeled this principle by spending roughly 90 percent of His life working an honest job as a simple carpenter. His example, along with the teaching of Scripture regarding work, helped to create the Protestant work ethic that has built America into the most productive and prosperous nation on the earth.

JESUS AND MEDICINE

In the world of pre-Christian Rome, hospitals were only for soldiers, gladiators, and slaves. Sadly, laborers and the poor had no medical options for their care.

This was transformed by Jesus. Jesus was called "the Great Physician" who healed people.[a] Luke (who wrote Luke and Acts) was a Christian doctor and recorded many of the miraculous healings that Jesus performed on the bodies of those who were sick and dying. Christian ministry included concern for the human body as a gift from God. In A.D. 325, the Council of Nicaea decreed that hospitals were to be established wherever there was a Christian church. Today, many hospitals have Christian origins, including Baptist, Presbyterian, and Catholic names. Internationally, the Red Cross continues its medical ministry, thanks to its founding by Christian Henri Dunant.

JESUS AND CHARITY

Jesus was poor and often spoke of His heart for the poor.[b] Additionally, Jesus also cared for the poor in practical ways, such as providing food for the hungry.[c]

It is not surprising that even the most ardent unbelievers agree that people who worship Jesus tend to be more generous in their charitable giving. Arthur C. Brooks, professor at Syracuse University and director of the Nonprofit Studies Program for the Maxwell School of Citizenship and Public Affairs, has researched the issue and concluded that religious conservatives donate more money to all sorts of charitable causes, regardless of income, than their liberal and secular counterparts.[158]

Brooks says, "These are not the sort of conclusions I ever thought I would reach when I started looking at charitable giving in graduate school, 10 years ago…I have to admit I probably would have hated what I have to say in this book."[159]

The book goes on to point out that his research confirms

----

[a] Luke 4:23; 5:31 [b] Luke 4:23; 5:31 [c] Matt 14:14-21; 15:32-38

that religious people give more than their secular counterparts in every possible way. This includes everything from volunteer hours to donating blood.

JESUS AND THE ARTS

More books have been written about Jesus than anyone who has ever lived. In the world of literature, the undeniable influence of the Christian faith appears in the works of Dante, Chaucer, Donne, Dostoevsky, Bunyan, Milton, Dickens, Hans Christian Andersen, Tolstoy, T.S. Eliot, C.S. Lewis, Tolkien, Sayers, and Solzhenitsyn.

Michaelangelo, Raphael, and Leonardo da Vinci were inspired by Christian faith and depicted Jesus in some of their artistic work. Cathedrals and churches around the world have also been beautifully built in His honor.

Musicians Bach, Handel, and Vivaldi claimed to be worshipers of Jesus. Today, an entire genre of worship music devoted to Jesus fills airwaves, stadiums, and churches with people singing about Him and singing to Him.

Regarding Jesus' impact on the arts, historian Philip Schaff said, "He has set more pens in motion and furnished themes for more sermons, orations, discussions, works of art, learned volumes, and sweet songs of praise than the whole army of great men of ancient and modern times."[160]

JESUS AND MERCY

No one has inspired more good than Jesus Christ. A *Newsweek* article said,

Because Christianity's influence is so pervasive throughout much of the world, it is easy to forget how radical its beliefs once were. Jesus' resurrection forever changed Christians' view of death. Rodney Stark, sociologist... points out that when a major plague hit the ancient Roman Empire, Christians had surprisingly high survival rates. Why? Most Roman citizens would banish any plague-stricken person from their household. But because Christians had no fear of death, they nursed their sick instead of throwing them out on the streets, not fearing death because of their certainty in eternal life. Therefore, many Christians survived the plague.[161]

Since Jesus was technically adopted by Joseph and grew up to care for the widow, orphan, and outcast, Christians have always had a heart for the poor and powerless. Historian and member of the American Antiquarian Society W. E. H. Lecky said,

> The character of Jesus has not only been the highest pattern of virtue, but the strongest incentive in its practice, and has exerted so deep an influence, that it may be truly said that the simple record of three years of active life has done more to regenerate and to soften mankind than all the disquisitions of philosophers and all the exhortations of moralists.[162]

JESUS AND ATROCITIES

In fairness, some horrible and wicked evils have been done by people who claim to be serving the cause of Christ.[163]

Let's look at some startling facts. During the 20th century alone, some 170 million people were killed by other human beings.[164]

Of those, roughly 130 million people died at the hands of those holding an atheistic ideology.[165] For example, Stalin killed 40 million people, Hitler killed six million Jews and nine to 10 million others (mainly Christians)[166], and Mao killed some 70 million Chinese. In addition to this number could be added the more than one billion people worldwide who were aborted and killed in the wombs of their mothers during the 20th century alone.

Comparatively, roughly 17 million people were killed by professing Christians in the name of Christ in 20 total centuries of Christian history. No Christian today lauds them or calls them heroes. Rather, we condemn their misguided zeal. So, in all of history, those proclaiming but possibly not professing Christian faith have killed only a tiny fraction of the number of people that atheists and followers of other religions have killed in one century.

Regarding the sins of Christianity, at least three things deserve mention. First, without excusing the sins committed by those who profess to be Christians, statistically atheism, which denies God and judgment from God, has been the source of far more atrocities than any religion, including Christianity. Second, not everyone who claims to be a Christian is in fact a Christian. Jesus Himself taught that Christians would be known by the fruit of love in their life.[a] He also said that on the day of judgment, many people will be surprised to find that they are not, in fact, Christians before being sent to Hell for their life of sin.[b] Third, Christians who sin are betraying Jesus and doing the very things He forbids them to do.

In summary, Jesus' legacy is truly without peer.

Jesus never ran for a political office, but more people have chosen Him to be their leader than anyone else who has ever lived.

Jesus was not formally educated, nor did he lecture in a classroom, but He has more students than anyone else ever has or will have.

Jesus was not a therapist, but He has helped more people than all the counselors, therapists, and psychologists combined. Jesus was not an artist, but more artwork has been commissioned of Him than of anyone else who has ever lived.

Truly, the difference Jesus has made in history is staggering. Even more endearing is the difference Jesus makes in our personal history. Billions of people on the earth have their own testimony of the difference Jesus has made in their life. Their stories are absolutely amazing— they are the people Jesus has loved, saved, forgiven, healed, restored, encouraged, empowered, and utterly transformed!

----
[a] Matt 5:43-46; 22:37-39; John 13:34-35 [b] Matt. 25:31-46

CHAPTER 11
WHAT WILL JESUS' KINGDOM BE LIKE WHEN HE RETURNS?

Amen. Come, Lord Jesus! –Revelation 22:20b

In our study of Jesus Christ as King of Kings, we have looked back at His life, death, burial, and Resurrection.

Now, we will look at His present and future.

What is Jesus doing today?

What will Jesus be doing in the future?

After Jesus rose from death and spent 40 days publicly proving His Resurrection, Acts 1 records what happened next and what would happen at the end of human history. Jesus' disciples asked if it was "time to restore the kingdom." Jesus said that before the Kingdom of God came, the Holy Spirit would descend and remain on the Church, empowering believers to evangelize the nations. Then,

> ...when he had said these things, as they were looking on, he was lifted up, and a cloud took him out of their sight. And while they were gazing into heaven as he went, behold, two men stood by them in white robes, and said, "Men of Galilee, why do you stand looking into heaven? This Jesus, who was taken up from you into heaven, will come in the same way as you saw him go into heaven."[a]

What a sight that must have been. Jesus' friends and followers watched Him ascend back to Heaven where He had come down from and were told that their little group would be part of the biggest global movement in history, bringing the good news of Jesus Christ to the nations of the earth! A few thousand years later, the Church of Jesus Christ stands as proof that the angelic promise was true, as Christianity is the biggest movement in world history, and the Holy Spirit has been faithful in every generation.

JESUS IS KING AND PRIEST

The Old Testament prophesied that Jesus would rule in

---

[a] Acts 1:9-11

glory with a king's scepter.[a] Jesus' mocking enemies revealed His Kingship when they pressed a crown of thorns into His head and hung over it the sign, "Jesus of Nazareth, the King of the Jews."[b]

Today, the risen Christ is ruling as King of Kings and Lord of Lords. Peering into the unseen realm, the book of Revelation no less than 45 times reveals Jesus seated upon a throne, reigning as sovereign King with a Kingdom destined to rule over all creation. Truth and judgment come from His throne while worship, praise, glory, and adoration go to His throne. By placing the throne of Jesus Christ at the center of creation and history, God radically displaces humanity; the goal of redemption and Kingdom is to orient all worship toward Jesus in glory alone.

Not only is Jesus currently reigning as King, but He is also serving as Priest. Jesus' ministry was not just happening a few thousand years ago; it continues today as He ministers on earth from His throne.

In the Old Testament, the priest would humbly stand between God and people as a mediator of sorts. He would bring the hopes, dreams, fears, and sins of the people before God as their advocate and intercessor. He would hear their confession of sin and pray for them. Furthermore, offering sacrifices was central to his role, to show that sin was very real and deserved death, while asking God for gracious forgiveness. Then he would speak God's blessing on the people. All the functions of the priest are ultimately fulfilled in Jesus, especially in the book of Hebrews.

In Hebrews, Jesus is our "high priest."[c] Not only is Jesus a priest superior to the Old Testament priests, but His sacrifice is also superior to theirs—He gave his own life and shed His own blood for our sin.[d] Jesus is alive today and ministers to us as our high priest who intercedes for us before God the Father.[e] Jesus' priestly intercession makes both our prayer and worship possible. We pray and worship the Father through Jesus our priest by the indwelling power of God the Holy Spirit, who

---

[a] Genesis 49:10; Zech. 9:9 cf. John 12:14–15 [b] Matt. 27:37; Mark 15:26; Luke 23:38; John 19:19 [c] Heb. 3:1; 4:14 [d] Heb. 9:26 [e] Heb. 7:2

has made our bodies the new temples in which He lives on the earth.

When we understand Jesus as our priest, we know that He loves us affectionately, tenderly, and personally. Furthermore, Jesus' desire for us is only good, and His ministry results in nothing less than life-changing intimacy with God the Father. Jesus makes new life and obedience possible by His loving, compassionate, and patient service to us as a faithful priest.

In his role as priest, Jesus is different from all other man-made religions and their false portraits of God. Virtually every religion sees God in a harsh way. Jesus is the only God who gets off His throne to humbly serve us and give us grace and mercy. As our Priest and King, Hebrews 4:15–16 says Jesus' throne is open to Christians:

> For we do not have a high priest who is unable to sympathize with our weaknesses, but one who in every respect has been tempted as we are, yet without sin. Let us then with confidence draw near to the throne of grace, that we may receive mercy and find grace to help in time of need.

Thus, Jesus is sympathetic to our temptations, weakness, suffering, sickness, disappointment, pain, confusion, loneliness, betrayal, brokenness, mourning, and sadness. Jesus does not refrain from entering our sick, fallen, and crooked world. Instead, He humbly came into this world to feel what we feel and face what we face, while remaining sinless. Subsequently, Jesus can both sympathize with and deliver us. Practically, this means that, in our time of need, we can run to Jesus, our sympathetic priest, who lives to serve us and give us grace and mercy for anything that life brings. Jesus' past ministry continues today, and He is available to you right now. One day, He will return as promised and bring His Kingdom with Him.

HOW IS OUR KING JESUS CHRIST A LION AND LAMB?

Most Christians view Jesus Christ as either Lion or Lamb,

but not both. Those with more lamb personalities focus on the parts of the Bible where Jesus was meek, kind, patient, loving, and appeared more passive or even timid. Those with more lion personalities will focus on the parts of the Bible where Jesus was strong, firm, urgent, and controversial, and appeared more active, if not aggressive.

Are you more of a lion or a lamb? Do you see Jesus more as a Lion or a Lamb?

The Bible presents Jesus as both a Lion and a Lamb. Looking into eternity, Revelation 5:5-6 says, "Weep no more; behold, the *Lion* of the tribe of Judah, the Root of David, has conquered, so that he can open the scroll and its seven seals. And between the throne and the four living creatures and among the elders I saw a *Lamb* standing, as though it had been slain, with seven horns and with seven eyes, which are the seven spirits of God sent out into all the earth."

A lion is the king of the jungle. Sometimes Jesus is a Lion. Examples include His repeated wars with Satan, fights with demonic religious leaders, and making a whip to attack money changers at the Temple for exchanging the worship of God for the demon god of money, Mammon. As a lion, Jesus Christ is tough.

Lambs are meek creatures who stick together with their flock because they are very social animals. We witness Jesus as Lamb in His tender love for women, children, the outcast, and those who are suffering. Examples include the healing of Jairus' daughter, forgiving the sinful Samaritan woman at the well, weeping at the death of His friend Lazarus, and tenderly caring for His mother Mary from the cross. As a lamb, Jesus Christ is tender.

Those who see Jesus more as Lion struggle with God forgiving and saving some people they struggle to forgive. Those who see Jesus more as Lamb struggle with God not loving, saving, and forgiving everyone forever.

Jesus is both tough as a Lion and tender as a Lamb. In Heaven, King Jesus will rule as a tender Lamb. In Hell, King Jesus will rule as a tough Lion.

When King Jesus returns, believers will experience Him

forever as a Lamb, and unbelievers will experience Him forever as a Lion.

For Christians, the change that Jesus brings into our life is perfectly and eternally completed when He returns. As we await the return of Jesus Christ, we will examine what will happen when that glorious day comes.

JESUS WILL LIFT THE CURSE AND ITS EFFECTS

The effects of the entrance of sin into the world through our first parents in Genesis 3 are many because of the curse. In Ecclesiastes, the word "toil" is often used to explain what life is like on the earth under the curse. Subsequently, life on the earth feels like a frantic and exhausting goose chase where there is no goose. This is because we are cursed. The curse serves to remind us that we are sinners and that we need our sin to be forgiven through the First Coming of Jesus, and we also need the curse to be lifted at the Second Coming of Jesus. Ecclesiastes 7:13 rightly asks, "Consider the work of God: who can make straight what he has made crooked?" Indeed, the world is a crooked place, and we crooked people cannot straighten out all that God himself has made crooked. Thankfully, Jesus is coming, and when He does, He will straighten us and everything else out by lifting the curse: "No longer will there be anything accursed..."[a]

Just imagine, for a moment, what it will be like when there is no curse. No one will get sick or die. Things will not continue to atrophy, break, and fall apart. All oppression, mental illness, physical pain, emotional distress, frustration, fear, anxiety, and conflict will be gone forever. Everything negative about this fallen world will end, and all the best parts of life on the earth will be improved and perfected. 1 Corinthians 2:9 says this coming reality is not just better than we think but even better than we can think, saying, "...no eye has seen, nor ear heard, nor the heart of man imagined, what God has prepared for those who love him..."

---

[a] Rev. 22:3

JESUS WILL GIVE EVERYONE GLORIFIED, RESURRECTED BODIES

The Scriptures are clear that sin leads to death.[a] The overturning of death is resurrection.

1 Corinthians 15 is the most extended treatment of resurrection in Scripture. It begins by investigating the Resurrection of Jesus, and then moves on to explain how His Resurrection is prototypical for all whose faith is in Him. Paul responds to two questions the Corinthian church and most churches since have asked about the resurrection body of Christians: how are the dead raised, and with what kind of body do they come?[b]

Paul answers the second question using an agricultural metaphor to explain what will happen to our body upon death.[c] Much like a seed that is buried in the ground dies and then springs forth as something more glorious than could have previously been, when a person dies, they too are buried but will likewise spring forth with a glorified resurrection body. Paul then assures us that, if God could create the sun, moon, stars, planets, animal life, plant life, and human life, He can certainly take our dead bodies and resurrect us in glorified new bodies.

Paul then seeks to explain the nature of our glorified resurrection bodies in greater detail.[d] First, our body is mortal and subject to sin and death in this life; the glorified body is not. Second, while our mortal body dies in dishonor, it will be raised in honor. Our body is in some ways like clothing that covers our immaterial spirit. God will, in essence, exchange our current physical covering for a new and more glorious eternal body. Quoting Genesis 2:7, Paul then says that just as our mortal body is patterned after Adam's death, our glorified body will be patterned after Jesus' Resurrection.[e]

The first question is then answered in verses 50–57. Our mortal bodies, marked by sin and death, are not fit for eternity.[f] Therefore, God must change our bodies to make them eternal.

---

[a] Gen 2:16-17; Rom 6:23 [b] 1 Cor 15:35-58 [c] 1 Cor 15:36-41 [d] 1 Cor 15:42-44 [e] 1 Cor 15:45-49
[f] 1 Corinthians 15:50

Paul then says that, because of our sin, we die.[a] Jesus came to conquer our sin through His death and conquer our death through His Resurrection. While both unbelievers and believers will be resurrected, they will not spend forever in the same place. Daniel 12:2 says, "...those who sleep in the dust of the earth shall awake, some to everlasting life [Kingdom of God], and some to shame and everlasting contempt [Hell]."

JESUS WILL PUNISH NON-CHRISTIANS IN HELL ACCORDING TO THEIR WICKEDNESS

When a great injustice has occurred, there is joy when justice is served. This explains why celebration rises when a dangerous criminal is captured, or a demonic dictator is toppled. Because God made us in His image with a conscience, we long for righteousness where wrongs are made right. In legal theory, "just deserts" states that, for there to be true justice, the punishment must fit the crime. This is precisely how Hell is ruled, according to the Bible.

Hell is where unrepentant and unforgiven sinners get perfect eternal justice.

Just as Jesus said that believers store up treasures for themselves, so unbelievers similarly store up wrath for themselves in Hell. Paul even uses the same Greek word as Jesus to contrast the judgment of believers and unbelievers.[b] Romans 2:6-8,11 warns of the damnation of unbelievers, saying,

> He will render to each one according to his works: to those who by patience in well-doing seek for glory and honor and immortality, he will give eternal life; but for those who are self-seeking and do not obey the truth, but obey unrighteousness, there will be wrath and fury...For God shows no partiality.

Jesus said, "Whoever believes in the Son has eternal life; whoever does not obey the Son shall not see life, but the wrath

---

[a] 1 Cor 15:51-57 [b] Matt. 6:19; Rom. 2:5

of God remains on him."[a] The new creation can be new only if everyone in it loves God and obeys Him. There can be no sin or sinners. They must be separated out, much like in our own day, where prisons keep criminals from harming others. In the Kingdom, the twin sins of idolatry and injustice will be transformed into obedience to Jesus' twin commands to love God and neighbor.[b]

A day is coming when God will judge the living and the dead[c] through the Son.[d] When the Son of Man's throne arrives on the earth, all will stand before Him for judgment.[e] From the beginning of creation[f] to the end[g], the Bible makes it clear that the basis of God's judgment is our deeds.[h]

There are degrees of punishment in Hell like there are degrees of reward in Heaven. Jesus told the people of Capernaum that it would be worse for them in the judgment than for Sodom.[i] The one who sins knowingly and willfully will receive a more severe beating than the one who did not know.[j] Both in life and in Hell, some sins receive more severe punishment because that is just.[k] This fits the scriptural teaching that some sins are qualitatively worse than others in that the depth of their evil and the damage that ensues is greater. Jesus illustrated this when he told Pilate, "...he who delivered me over to you has the greater sin."[l]

WHAT DOES SCRIPTURE TEACH ABOUT HELL?

Jesus talks about Hell more than anyone else in all of Scripture. Jesus' words come in the context of the rest of Scripture, which says that God "desires all people to be saved and to come to the knowledge of the truth."[m] Furthermore, He "is patient toward you, not wishing that any should perish, but that all should reach repentance."[n] Jesus said more about Hell than about any other topic. Amazingly, 13 percent of his sayings are about Hell and judgment; more than half of His

---

[a] John 3:36 [b] Deut. 6:5; 10:12; 30:6; Lev. 19:18; Matt. 22:37–40; Mark 12:30–31; Luke 10:27; Rom. 13:9–10; 15:2; Gal. 5:14; 6:10; James 2:8 [c] Acts 10:42; 2 Tim. 4:1; 1 Pet. 4:5 [d] Ps. 2:12; Mark 14:62; John 5:22; Acts 17:31 [e] Matt. 25:31–46; Rev. 20:11–15 [f] Gen. 2:15–17 [g] Rev. 20:12–13 [h] Jer. 17:10; 32:19; Matt. 16:27; Rom. 2:6; Gal. 6:7–8; Rev. 2:23; 22:12 [i] Matt. 11:21–24 [j] Luke 12:47–48 [k] Num. 15:22–30; Lev. 4:1–35; 5:15–19; Matt. 18:6; 1 Tim. 5:8; James 3:1; 1 John 5:16–18 [l] John 19:11 [m] 1 Tim. 2:4 [n] 2 Pet. 3:9

parables relate to the eternal judgment of sinners.[167]

The Bible does not give us a detailed exposition of Hell, but there are many descriptions of the fate of its inhabitants in this place of eternal punishment. They include (1) fire[a]; (2) darkness[b]; (3) punishment[c]; (4) exclusion from God's presence[d]; (5) restlessness[e]; (6) second death[f]; and (7) weeping and gnashing of teeth.[g]

Hell is not a fun place where sinners get to live out their sinful pleasures, as if Satan rules over Hell and sin can be pursued without inhibition. This erroneous view of Satan ruling in Hell comes not from Scripture but from Puritan John Milton's *Paradise Lost*, which has the devil arrogantly declaring, "Better to reign in hell, then serve in Heav'n."[168] Satan will not reign there. Hell is a place of punishment that God prepared for the devil and his angels.[h] Hell is where the damned

> ...will drink the wine of God's wrath, poured full strength into the cup of His anger, and...be tormented with fire and sulfur in the presence of the holy angels and in the presence of the Lamb. And the smoke of their torment goes up forever and ever, and they have no rest, day or night...[i]

Jesus rules Hell as much as He rules Heaven because Jesus Christ is Lord over all.

At the end of the age, the devil will be "thrown into the lake of fire and sulfur where the beast and the false prophet were, and they will be tormented day and night forever and ever."[j] Hell will be ruled by Jesus, and humans and demons alike, including Satan, will be tormented there continually.

Hell is real and terrible. It is eternal. There is no possibility of amnesty or reprieve. Daniel says the dead will be resurrected "to shame and everlasting contempt."[k] Jesus says, "Depart from me, you cursed, into the eternal fire prepared for the devil and

---

[a] Matt. 13:42, 50; 18:8, 9; Rev. 19:20; 20:14–15 [b] Matt. 25:30; Jude 13 [c] Rev. 14:10–11 [d] Matt. 7:23; 25:41; Luke 16:19ff.; 2 Thess. 1:9 [e] Rev. 14:11 [f] Rev. 2:11; 20:6, 14; 21:8 [g] Matt. 13:42, 50; 22:12–13; 24:51; 25:30; Luke 13:28 [h] Matt. 25:41 [i] Rev. 14:10–11 [j] Rev. 20:10 [k] Dan. 12:2

his angels…And these will go away into eternal punishment…"[a]
Paul tells us,

> …God considers it just to repay with affliction those who
> afflict you, and to grant relief to you who are afflicted as
> well as to us, when the Lord Jesus is revealed from heaven
> with his mighty angels in flaming fire, inflicting vengeance
> on those who do not know God and on those who do not
> obey the gospel of our Lord Jesus. They will suffer the
> punishment of eternal destruction, away from the presence
> of the Lord and from the glory of his might…[b]

Perhaps the clearest and most gripping depiction of Hell
is "Gehenna." The name refers to an area outside of the city of
Jerusalem where idolatry and horrendous sin, including child
sacrifice, were practiced.[c] Gehenna was a place so despised and
cursed by God's people that they turned it into the city dump
where the dead bodies of criminals were stacked. Jesus spoke
of Gehenna as the hellish final home of the wicked.[d] Since
Gehenna is described as a fiery abyss[e], clearly it is also the lake
of fire[f] to which all the godless will ultimately be eternally
sentenced[g] together with Satan, demons, and unrepentant
sinners.[h] So, when the Bible speaks of Hell as a place where the
fire is not quenched and the worm does not die, the original
hearers would easily have remembered Gehenna, where this
reality was ever present outside of their city.[i]

Our attitude toward Hell should be the same as that of the
Father, who takes no pleasure in the death of the wicked but
begs them to turn from their evil ways.[j] Jesus joins the Father's
compassionate yearning as He weeps over Jerusalem.[k] Paul also
has "great sorrow and unceasing anguish in my heart. For I
could wish that I myself were accursed and cut off from Christ
for the sake of my brothers, my kinsmen according to the
flesh."[l] Furthermore, he "did not cease night or day to admonish

---
[a] Matt. 25:41, 46 [b] 2 Thess. 1:6–9 [c] 2 Kings 16:3; 21:6; 2 Chron. 28:3; 33:6; Jer. 19:56; 32:35
[d] Matt. 5:22; 10:28; 18:9 [e] Mark 9:43 [f] Matt. 13:42, 50 [g] Matt. 23:15, 33 [h] Matt. 25:41; Rev.
19:20; 20:10, 14, 15 [i] Isa. 66:24; Mark 9:47–48 [j] Ezek. 18:23; 33:11; 1 Tim. 2:4; 2 Pet. 3:9
[k] Jer. 31:20; Hos. 11:8; Matt. 23:37–38; Luke 19:41–44 [l] Rom. 9:2–3

everyone with tears."ᵃ

Feeling as he ought about Hell, legendary preacher Charles Spurgeon rightly began his sermon on the eternal conscious torment of the wicked in Hell this way: "Beloved, these are such weighty things that while I dwell upon them I feel far more inclined to sit down and weep than to stand up and speak to you."[169]

DID JESUS GO TO HELL AFTER HE DIED ON THE CROSS?

It has been wrongly taught by some that following His death on the cross, Jesus went to Hell for three days. Building on this error, some have even said that Jesus was tormented by Satan in Hell in the time between His crucifixion and Resurrection. It is easily cleared up by a faithful reading of Scripture. First, Jesus paid the penalty for our sins on the cross and said His work was "finished."ᵇ Therefore, there was nothing else to be done for us, such as going to Hell to suffer for our sins yet again.ᶜ

Second, Jesus told us from the cross where He was going ("today you will be with me in Paradise"ᵈ, which was not Hell. Third, Revelation 20:11-15 explains that, at the end of time, Hades (the holding place for unbelievers) will be opened up and unbelievers will be judged before they are sent into the lake of fire, which is Hell and the second death. Until that time, which we are still awaiting, no one, including Jesus, is in Hell. Fourth, at no time does Satan ever rule over Jesus, even in Hell. We see in Revelation 14:10 that Jesus Christ rules over Hell, and in Revelation 20:10 that Jesus rules over the punishment of Satan and demons in Hell.

The earliest version of the Apostles' Creed (roughly A.D. 140) did not have the phrase "He descended into hell" and neither did the Nicene Creed (roughly A.D. 325). Most scholars believe that the phrase was a later addition, perhaps

---

ᵃ Acts 20:31; cf. Acts 20:19–20; Phil. 3:18 ᵇ John 19:30 ᶜ 2 Cor 5:21; Col 2:13-15 ᵈ Luke 23:43

around A.D. 390. In Greek, this added phrase is κατελθόντα εἰς τὰ κατώτατα, (*"katelthonta eis ta katôtata"*) meaning "descended to the lower place or into the grave," representing the biblical truth that Jesus' body was buried.[a]

JESUS WILL REWARD CHRISTIANS IN HEAVEN ACCORDING TO THEIR RIGHTEOUSNESS

Christians will not be judged at the end of this life in the same way that non-Christians will be. The Bible teaches this truth clearly and repeatedly. Jesus said, "Truly, truly, I say to you, whoever hears my word and believes him who sent me has eternal life. He does not come into judgment, but has passed from death to life."[b] Paul says, "There is therefore now no condemnation for those who are in Christ Jesus."[c] Simply stated, in Christ, all sin is forgiven, having been judged at Jesus' cross.[d] Subsequently, Christians are members of the family of God now and forever.

Nonetheless, Christians will be judged at the end of this life in a way that is different from the judgment of non-Christians. This life, and what we do and do not do with it, matters greatly. The Holy Spirit has given every Christian time, talent, and treasure that they are to steward well for the Kingdom. The Christian's judgment is a day of assessment when "...we must all appear before the judgment seat of Christ, so that each one may receive what is due for what he has done in the body, whether good or evil."[e]

This theme of accountability and reward runs all through Scripture as a continual reminder not to waste our life but rather steward it in light of eternity.[f]

To illustrate this concept, Jesus tells a Kingdom story in which believers receive 10 minas, a large amount of money, and they're commanded to do business with it.[g] The servant who brings 10 more minas receives authority over 10 cities in the kingdom, while the servant who brings five minas receives

---

[a] 1 Cor. 15:4 [b] John 5:24 [c] Romans 8:1 [d] Col. 2:13; 1 John 2:12 [e] 2 Cor. 5:10 [f] Matt. 24:45–47; 25:14–30; Luke 12:42–48; 16:1–13; 17:7–10; 19:12–27; Rom. 2:16; 14:10; 1 Cor. 3:8–15; 4:5; 9:17–27; Col. 3:23–25; 1 Tim. 2:3–6; 2 Tim. 4:8; 1 Pet. 1:7; 5:4; Rev. 4:4, 10; 22:12 [g] Luke 19:12–27

authority over five. The last servant, who hides his mina from fear of the master, typifies someone who does not have a grace relationship with Jesus. Though his description of the Master shows that he does not know God at all, God in His lavish grace still endows him with a mina, a large amount of money. The point of Jesus' story is that if we are truly Christians and know the love of our Master, we should faithfully invest our lives in the service of His Kingdom. The quality of work we do will be revealed and tested in the end, and only work that survives Jesus' evaluation will be worthy of a reward. Positively, our day of testing can be a day of great rejoicing when we hear Jesus declare, "Well done," if we are faithful stewards in this life.

Negatively, some Christians will be grieved by the lack of reward given to them. 1 Corinthians 3:15 says, "If anyone's work is burned up, he will suffer loss, though he himself will be saved, but only as through fire." The Bible is clear that there are eternal consequences for believers doing both good and evil. 2 Corinthians 5:10 says, "For we must all appear before the judgment seat of Christ, so that each one may receive what is due for what he has done in the body, whether good or evil."

Those who love Jesus will strive to be like Him. Because we are God's workmanship, created for good works, we should do them.[a] The Bible repeatedly exhorts us to "make every effort" to be faithful to God's calling.[b]

While we do not know exactly what our eternal rewards will be, it should comfort a believer that the injustice and loss we have suffered in this life will be repaid by God. Furthermore, since most people invest in some sort of retirement account, it should be motivating for us to store up our treasures in Heaven by giving generously, serving faithfully, and suffering dutifully, knowing that Jesus Christ will deposit all those things into our eternal account.

WHAT DOES SCRIPTURE TEACH ABOUT HEAVEN?

Most people don't know much about Heaven, and what

---

[a] Eph. 2:10 [b] Luke 13:24; Rom. 14:19; Eph. 4:3; Heb. 4:11; 12:14; 2 Pet. 1:5–10; 3:14

they think is often just plain wrong. Based upon some bad religious art in the Sistine Chapel, the average person thinks of Heaven as the boring place where we're all pretending not to be miserable as chubby babies sitting on clouds wearing diapers plunking harps for all eternity.

According to the Bible, there is one reality ruled by God over two realms. One realm is the spirit world where God, divine beings (including angels), and departed saints live right now. The other realm is the physical world where human beings live right now.

Originally, these two realms were connected. The Garden of Eden in Genesis was literally Heaven on earth, where the unseen realm and seen realm connected. This explains why Adam and Eve met with God there, were not shocked when a divine being showed up (Satan), and saw an angel keep them from the Tree of Life once they sinned. Once we sinned, the realms were disconnected. So, upon death, the two parts of our being are also disconnected. Our body goes into the ground awaiting resurrection. Our soul goes to be with God.

The apostle Paul says this is "far better" than our current life on earth and all we have is "gain" to look forward to being "at home with the Lord."[a] So, if someone loves Jesus and dies today, they are with Jesus in the spiritual Heaven. That, however, is not their final destination. When Jesus returns to earth, He brings Heaven to earth with Him to restore things to how they were before sin entered the world. Those who love Jesus will be joined to their resurrection bodies to live forever on the New Earth. Far too many people think of Heaven only in terms of the intermediate spiritual state and not the earthly physical reality that God has planned for all eternity, as we studied in a previous chapter.

Right now, Heaven exists in the unseen realm and is just as real as the world we occupy in the seen realm. Much like a Zoom call, Isaiah, Ezekiel, and John all got to communicate with Heaven and see what was happening there. Revelation 6:9-11 says, "I saw...the souls of those who had been slain for the

_____
[a] 2 Cor. 5:8; Php. 1:21-23

word of God and for the witness they had borne. They cried out with a loud voice, 'O Sovereign Lord, holy and true, how long before you will judge and avenge our blood on those who dwell on the earth?' Then they were each given a white robe and told to rest a little longer..."

The departed Christians right now are consciously aware of what is happening both in Heaven and on earth. Additionally, they communicate with God and one another. This is an amazing insight.

When we think of Heaven, we need to stop thinking about leaving this planet and instead think about what it will be like when Jesus' prayer is answered, the Kingdom comes to earth, and God's will is done from one end of the cosmos to the other. God does not abandon His design plan from creation. God will not be defeated, dissuaded, or distracted. God remains focused on going back to where He started and sticking with His plan to have human life flourishing on earth and ruled by Heaven, which comes to earth.

Even though we change, and Heaven and earth change, God does not change, and God does not change His plan for His people and His planet. This explains why the Bible uses lots of words like restore, redeem, resurrect, renew, etc. Acts 3:21 looks forward to "the time for restoring all the things about which God spoke by the mouth of his holy prophets..." God will go back to where He started to lift the curse, sentence Satan, raise the dead, and make the realm of Eden in the unseen world visible in the seen realm of earth. He will overtake and liberate all that has been cursed by our sin to be cured by His Son.

The analogy that Paul uses for life as we experience it right now is childbirth. We've never met a woman who likes the process of childbirth, though we've met many women who love the child they birthed. For this Christian, this life of screaming, weeping, stressing, and pushing is our version of birth where God will bring new, beautiful, and worthwhile life on the other side. Like childbirth, this painful process is worth the new life birthed on the other side of all the pain. For the Christian, this frames our love for Heaven and infuses our present pain with incredible meaning, as one day we will have the same joy as a new mom holding her baby.

Right now, there is a place called Heaven that exists in the unseen realm. Living there are God, divine beings including angels, and departed saints who loved Jesus in their life on earth. When you die, you go there to be with them if you love Jesus. Theologians call this the "intermediate heaven."

One day, maybe in hours or centuries, Jesus Christ will return to this sin-cursed, tear-soaked world with Heaven as the King, and everyone and everything in His Kingdom will make the big move to New Earth. Just as Jesus brought Heaven and earth together at His first coming, He will bring the New Heaven and New Earth together at His Second Coming.[a]

There are six ways that the Bible describes God's forever Kingdom, which the Bible often calls the New Earth: Sabbath, Kingdom, City, Home, Garden, and Party. For starters, you will need to use your imagination for each of these, but it is fun to imagine what this new forever reality will be like. Heaven is not just bigger and better than we think; it is bigger and better than we *can* think: "No eye has seen, no ear has heard, and no mind has imagined what God has prepared for those who love him."[b]

Through Jesus Christ, God is welcoming you to join Him in the Kingdom of God ruled by the King of Kings. There, you will have a perfect resurrected body like Jesus and do the things that you were created to do without sin, curse, Satan and demons, evil, sickness, or death. You will live as Adam and Eve lived before sin and the curse. You will have a physical body, explore creation, eat meals, create, explore, enjoy art, build perfect relationships, make memories, and enjoy perfection without sin, sinners, or Satan forever and ever.

ARE YOU GOING TO HELL OR HEAVEN?

After explaining Heaven and Hell, the closing verses of the Bible say, "Come!" This is God's invitation for you to receive

---

[a] Isa. 65:17; 2 Pet. 3:13; Rev. 21:1-3 [b] 1 Corinthians 2:9, NLT

Jesus Christ and begin to live under His reign as King of Kings.

We want this for you, and we would be unloving if we finished this book without seeking to ensure that you are a Christian.

Have you confessed your sins to Jesus Christ, seeking forgiveness and salvation? If not, asking Jesus to forgive your sin as your Savior and leading you through life as your Lord is what you should do in prayer right now by praying this simple prayer from the heart:

> *Lord Jesus, I acknowledge that I am a sinner.*
> *Lord Jesus, I believe that you are God who lived without sin,*
>   *died for my sin, and rose from death as my Savior.*
> *Lord Jesus, I repent of my sin, and receive you as my God,*
>   *Savior, and Lord over my life.*
> *Lord Jesus, I promise to now live as a Christian, growing*
>   *in my relationship with you by continually repenting of my*
>   *sin, reading the Bible, talking to you in prayer, and being*
>   *part of your family in a local church.*
> *Amen!*

If you prayed that prayer, please let a Christian family member or friend know, and find a good church near you to get involved in as a new member of God's forever family. We would also love to hear from you and pray for you if you would kindly email us at **hello@realfaith.com**.

One day, all the cultures of the earth will be gone, and only two cultures will remain—the culture of Heaven and the culture of Hell. Until Jesus returns, or you resurrect, you live between Heaven and Hell. Every day, the decisions you make will either pull the culture of Hell up into your life or invite the culture of Heaven down into your life by the Holy Spirit. Every decision you make will make your life feel more like Heaven or Hell. We would encourage you to keep looking to Jesus as Lord over all and making decisions that allow your life to answer His prayer in Matthew 6:10, "Your kingdom come, your will be done, on earth as it is in heaven." Until you get to Heaven, God wants Heaven to come to you!

ENDNOTES

1. https://www.penguinrandomhouse.ca/books/239838/the-greatest-words-ever-spoken-by-steven-k-scott/9781601426673/excerpt

2. Grant R. Osborne, *Revelation, Baker Exegetical Commentary on the New Testament* (Grand Rapids, MI: Baker Academic, 2002), 789.

3. For more, read Stephen Prothero's *American Jesus.*

4. "Who Was Jesus?" *Larry King Live.* First broadcast December 24, 2004, CNN, http://transcripts.cnn.com/TRANSCRIPTS/0412/24/lkl.01.html

5. Watch Tower Bible and Tract Society of Pennsylvania, "The Truth about Angels."

6. Douglas J. Davies, *An Introduction to Mormonism* (Cambridge: Cambridge University Press, 2003), 35.

7. Nichols, Mather, and Schmidt, *Encyclopedic Dictionary of Cults, Sects, and World Religions*, 195.

8. https://www.churchofjesuschrist.org/study/manual/gospel-topics/god-the-father?lang=eng

9. https://mormonchurch.com/587/do-mormons-believe-jesus-and-satan-are-brothers

10. https://speeches.byu.edu/talks/bruce-r-mcconkie/relationship-lord

11. Sinclair B. Ferguson and J.I. Packer, *New Dictionary of Theology* (Downers Grove, IL: InterVarsity Press, 2000), 474.

12. Ron Rhodes, *The Challenge of the Cults and New Religions* (Grand Rapids, MI: Zondervan, 2001), 276.

13. Levi Dowling, *The Aquarian Gospel of Jesus the Christ* (Santa Fe, NM: New Antlantean Press, 2004), 87.

14. Philip Swihart, *Reincarnation, Edgar Cayce, and the Bible* (Downers Grove, IL: InterVarsity, 1978), 18.

15. Dalai Lama, "The Karma of the Gospel," *Newsweek*, March 27, 2000.

16. Mahatma Gandhi, *Harijan* (March 6, 1937): 25.

17. https://www.pewresearch.org/religion/2015/04/02/

religious-projections-2010-2050/

18. Victoria Smithee, "Speaker Discusses Role of Christ in Islam," *The North Texas Daily* (September 14, 2006), http://www.ntdaily.com/media/storage/paper877/news/2006/09/14/news/2006/09/14/News/Speaker.Discusses.RoleOf.Christ.In.Islam-2271697.shtml.

19. Annemarie Schimmel, *Islam: An Introduction* (Albany, NY: State University of New York Press, 1992), 73.

20. Thich Nhat Hanh, *Living Buddha, Living Christ* (New York: Riverhead, 1995), xxi.

21. Billy Graham, "God's Hand on My Life," *Newsweek*, March 29, 1999, 65.

22. John A. Buehrens and Forrest Church, *A Chosen Faith: An Introduction to Unitarian Universalism* (Boston: Beacon, 1998), 7.

23. Watch Tower Bible and Tract Society of Pennsylvania, "Is God Always Superior to Jesus?" Should You Believe in the Trinity? Watchtower Society online ed., http://www.watchtower.org/e/ti/index.htm?article=article_06.htm.

24. *Science and Health*, Mary Baker Eddy, 361:11-13.

25. Quoted in Charles Edmund Deland, *The Mis-Trials of Jesus* (Boston, MA: Richard G. Badger, 1914), 118–19.

26. Craig L. Blomberg, *Matthew, The New American Commentary* (Nashville: Broadman, 1992), 315–16.

27. Jeff Chu, "10 Questions for Katharine Jefferts Schori," *Time* (July 10, 2006), http://www.time.com/time/magazine/article/ 0,9171,1211587-2,00.html.

28. https://www.dailymail.co.uk/sciencetech/article-14096551/earliest-inscription-jesus-god-israel-prison-ancient-discovery.html

29. C.S. Lewis, *Mere Christianity* (New York: Macmillan, 1952), 40-41.

30. Kenneth Samples, *Prophets of the Apocalypse: David Koresh and Other American Messiahs* (Grand Rapids, MI: Baker, 1994), 15, 59–60, 69–70.

31. Ibid., 70

32. https://journals.sagepub.com/doi/10.2466/pr0.1993.73.1.331

33. *The Passion: Religion and the Movies*, A&E Television and The History Channel.

34. Athanasius, "Orations Against the Arians," bk. 3, in Richard A. Norris, trans. and ed., *The Christological Controversy* (Philadelphia: Fortress, 1980), 92–93, emphasis in original.

35. Dallas Theological Seminary (2004; 2005). *Bibliotheca Sacra*, vol. 161 (vnp.161.641.75).

36. Stanley Grenz, David Guretzki, and Cherith Fee Nordling, *Pocket Dictionary of Theological Terms* (Downers Grove, IL: InterVarsity Press, 1999), 65.

37. For an excellent discussion of how there is complexity in the unity of God for first century Jews, see Richard J. Bauckham, *Jesus and the God of Israel: God Crucified and Other Studies on the New Testament's Christology of Divine Identity*, Eerdmans, 2008.

38. Ron Rhodes, *The Counterfeit Christ of the New Age Movement* (Grand Rapids, MI: Baker, 1990), 215.

39. George Eldon Ladd, *A Theology of the New Testament*, rev. ed. (Grand Rapids, MI: Eerdmans, 1993), 278.

40. Suetonius, *Life of the Deified Augustus*, Chapter 94.

41. D. Martyn Lloyd-Jones, *God the Father, God the Son* (Wheaton, IL: Crossway, 1996), 264.

42. James Orr, *The Virgin Birth of Christ* (New York: Scribner's, 1907), 138.

43. Creflo Dollar, *Changing Your World*, TBN, December 8, 2002, quoted in Bob Hunter, "Christianity Still in Crisis: A Word of Faith Update," *Christian Research Journal*, 30, no. 3 (2007): 16.

44. See Robert S. Birchard, *Cecil B. DeMille's Hollywood* (Lexington, KY: University Press of Kentucky, 2004).

45. Stephen Prothero, *American Jesus*, 94.

46. Sam Williams, "Toward a Theology of Emotion," *Southern Baptist Journal of Theology 7*, no. 4 (2003): 63.

47. Williams, "Toward a Theology of Emotion," 56.

48. Stephen Voorwinde, *Jesus' Emotions in the Gospels* (London; New York: T&T Clark, 2011), 2.

49. Ibid., 59.

50. Ibid., 119; In the Greek text, according to the Gramcord program, Luke has 19,496 words, Matthew 18,363, John 15,675, and Mark 11,313. (The Gramcord Grammatical Concordance System is based on the 26th edition of the Nestle-Aland Novum Testamentum Graece [Stuttgart: Deutsche Bibelgesellschaft, 1979]).
51. Ibid., 151.
52. Robert G. Hoeber, *Concordia Self-Study Bible*, electronic ed. (St. Louis, MO: Concordia Publishing House, 1997), Luke 22:44.
53. Elton Trueblood, *The Humor of Christ* (New York: Harper & Row, 1964), 10.
54. Ibid.,15.
55. Leland Ryken, James C. Wilhoit, and Tremper Longman III, eds., *Dictionary of Biblical Imagery*, s.v. "Jesus as Humorist," 410.
56. Trueblood, *The Humor of Christ*, 127.
57. Ryken, Wilhoit, and Longman, *Dictionary of Biblical Imagery*, s.v. "Humor—Jesus as Humorist," 410.
58. Quoted in G. C. Berkouwer, *The Person of Christ*, trans. John Vriend (Grand Rapids, MI: Eerdmans, 1954), 94.
59. Todd Miles, *Super Heroes Can't Save You*. B & H Academic, 2018.
60. Wilbur M. Smith, in Josh McDowell, *Evidence That Demands a Verdict, vol. 1* (San Bernardino, CA: Here's Life, 1992), 22.
61. J. Dwight Pentecost, *Prophecy for Today* (Grand Rapids, MI: Zondervan, 1971), 14–15.
62. Thomas Paine, "Examination of the Prophecies," in William M. Van der Weyde, ed., *The Life and Works of Thomas Paine, vol. 9* (New Rochelle, NY: Thomas Paine National Historical Association, 1925), 206.
63. Josh McDowell, *Evidence That Demands a Verdict*, 141.
64. Blaise Pascal, *Pensées*, trans. A. J. Krailsheimer (London: Penguin, 1966), 129.
65. Donald Bloesch, *Jesus Christ: Savior and Lord* (Downers Grove, IL: InterVarsity, 1997), 86.
66. https://www.churchofjesuschrist.org/study/ensign/1971/04/

the-king-follett-sermon?lang=eng

67. Robert Funk, *Honest to Jesus: Jesus for a New Millennium '* (New York: HarperCollins, 1996), 313.

68. J. Gresham Machen, *The Virgin Birth of Christ* (New York: Harper & Brothers, 1930), 382.

69. Ibid, 383.

70. *The Apology of Aristides*, trans. and ed. Rendel Harris (London: Cambridge University Press, 1893), 25.

71. Allen C. Myers ed., *The Eerdmans Bible Dictionary* (Grand Rapids, MI: Eerdmans, 1987), 207.

72. D. A. Carson, *The Gospel According to John* (Grand Rapids, MI: Wm. B. Eerdmans Publishing Company, 1991), 389.

73. James D. Tabor and Simcha Jacobovici, *The Jesus Discovery* (New York: Simon and Schuster Inc., 2012), 122.

74. https://www.newsweek.com/satan-getting-hot-hell-american-pop-culture-1790669

75. Robert H. Stein, "Fatherhood of God," in *Evangelical Dictionary of Biblical Theology*, electronic ed., Baker Reference Library (Grand Rapids: Baker Book House, 1996), 247.

76. Walter A. Elwell and Barry J. Beitzel, "Only Begotten," *Baker Encyclopedia of the Bible* (Grand Rapids, MI: Baker Book House, 1988), 1590.

77. Lloyd-Jones, *God the Father, God the Son*, 286–87.

78. Abraham Kuyper, *The Work of the Holy Spirit*, trans. Henri de Vries (Grand Rapids, MI: Eerdmans, 1975), 97.

79. Gerald F. Hawthorne, *The Presence and the Power: The Significance of the Spirit in the Life and Ministry of Jesus* (Dallas: Word, 1991), 234.

80. Ibid.

81. https://christiananswers.net/dictionary/miracle.html

82. John G. Butler, *Jesus Christ: His Miracles, vol. 2, Studies of the Savior* (Clinton, IA: LBC Publications, 2001), 14.

83. https://plato.stanford.edu/entries/miracles/

84. https://davidhume.org/texts/e/10

85. John G. Butler, *Jesus Christ: His Miracles, vol. 2, Studies of the Savior* (Clinton, IA: LBC Publications, 2001), 15.

86. Sanh. 43a.

87. Origen, *Contra Cels.* 1.38.
88. Flavius Josephus, "Jewish Antiquities," in *The New Complete Works of Josephus*, trans. William Whiston (Grand Rapids, MI: Kregel, 1999), 18.63.
89. Ronald D. Roberts, "Miracle," ed. John D. Barry et al., *The Lexham Bible Dictionary* (Bellingham, WA: Lexham Press, 2016).
90. Ibid.
91. Ibid.
92. Jonathan Warren P. (Pagán), "Providence and Miracles," in *Lexham Survey of Theology*, ed. Mark Ward et al. (Bellingham, WA: Lexham Press, 2018).
93. David A. Fiensy, "Crucifixion," in *The Lexham Bible Dictionary*, ed. John D. Barry et al. (Bellingham, WA: Lexham Press, 2016).
94. Ibid.
95. Much of the following historical overview of crucifixion is from A&E Television and The History Channel's two-hour special called *Crucifixion* (March 23, 2008).
96. https://www.dailymail.co.uk/news/article-13132065/ Beheadings-crucifixions-heads-spikes-Saudi-Arabia-executions-Crown-Prince.html
97. David A. Fiensy, "Crucifixion," in *The Lexham Bible Dictionary*, ed. John D. Barry et al. (Bellingham, WA: Lexham Press, 2016).
98. Ibid.
99. Ibid.
100. Suetonius, *The Lives of the Caesars,* Vesp. 5.4.
101. Josephus, J.W. 7.203.
102. Cicero, Pro Rabirio Perduellionis Reo 5.16
103. *Crucifixion*, A&E Television and The History Channel.
104. Ibid.
105. David A. Fiensy, "Crucifixion," in *The Lexham Bible Dictionary*, ed. John D. Barry et al. (Bellingham, WA: Lexham Press, 2016).
106. *Crucifixion*, A&E Television and The History Channel.
107. Luke 23:34; Luke 23:43; John 19:26-27, Psalm 22:2, Matt. 27:46 cf. Mark 15:34, as this is the only statement from the

cross appearing in more than one Gospel, John 19:28-29. It is possible that the sponge and wine vinegar were part of the military kit used by soldiers to clean themselves after going to the bathroom in the field, the ancient version of both toilet paper and disinfectant.

108. To learn more about each facet of the cross, see our book *Death by Love: Letters from the Cross* (Wheaton, IL: Crossway, 2008).

109. Eugene E. Carpenter and Philip W. Comfort, *Holman Treasury of Key Bible Words: 200 Greek and 200 Hebrew Words Defined and Explained* (Nashville, TN: Broadman & Holman Publishers, 2000), 370.

110. https://www.rasmussenreports.com/public_content/lifestyle/ holidays/most_americans_believe_in_resurrection_of_jesus

111. "Sleep," in Leland Ryken, Jim Wilhoit, et al., *Dictionary of Biblical Imagery* (Downers Grove, IL: InterVarsity, 2000), 799.

112. N.T. Wright, *The Resurrection of the Son of God* (Minneapolis: Fortress Press, 2003), 32.

113. Aeschylus, *Eumenides* 647-48, quoted in Wright, *Resurrection*, 32.

114. Wright, *Resurrection*, 35.

115. Ibid., 60.

116. Ibid., 76.

117. Craig spent two years as a fellow of the Humboldt Foundation studying the resurrection of Jesus Christ at the University of Munich. See William Lane Craig, *The Historical Argument for the Resurrection of Jesus During the Deist Controversy* (Lewiston, ID: Edwin Mellen, 1985), and *Assessing the New Testament Evidence for the Historicity of the Resurrection of Jesus* (Lewiston, ID: Edwin Mellen, 1989).

118. William Lane Craig, "Did Jesus Rise from the Dead?" in *Jesus Under Fire: Modern Scholarship Reinvents the Historical Jesus*, ed. Michael J. Wilkins and J. P. Moreland (Grand Rapids, MI: Zondervan, 1996), 160, emphases in original.

119. Edwin Yamauchi, "Easter: Myth, Hallucination, or History?" *Christianity Today*, March 15, 1974 and March 29, 1974, 4–7, 12–16.

120. Ibid.

121. Ibid.

122. See Lee Strobel, *The Case for the Real Jesus* (Grand Rapids, MI: Zondervan, 2007), 174–75; and Bruce M. Metzger, *Historical and Literary Studies: Pagan, Jewish, and Christian* (Grand Rapids, Eerdmans, 1968), 11.

123. See Craig, "Did Jesus Rise from the Dead?"

124. James Orr, *The Resurrection of Jesus* (London: Hodder & Stoughton, 1908), 198.

125. J. P. Moreland, *Scaling the Secular City* (Grand Rapids, MI: Baker, 1987), 172.

126. Quoted in Richard N. Ostling, "Who Was Jesus?" *Time*, August 15, 1988, 41.

127. William Lane Craig, *The Son Rises: The Historical Evidence for the Resurrection of Jesus* (Eugene, OR: Wipf & Stock, 2001), 134.

128. Ibid.

129. Simon Greenleaf, *The Testimony of the Evangelists: The Gospels Examined by the Rules of Evidence Administered in Courts of Justice* (Grand Rapids, MI: Kregel, 1995), 32.

130. Kenneth Scott Latourette, *A History of the Expansion of Christianity, 7 vols., The First Five Centuries* (New York: Harper, 1937), 1:59.

131. Lucian, "The Death of Peregrine," in *The Works of Lucian of Samosata*, trans. H. W. Fowler and F. G. Fowler, vol. 4 (Oxford: Clarendon, 1949), 11–13. Also see Pliny, Letters, trans. William Melmoth, vol. 2 (Cambridge: Harvard University Press, 1935), 10.96.

132. Murray J. Harris, *Raised Immortal: Resurrection and Immortality in the New Testament* (Grand Rapids, MI: Eerdmans, 1985), 40.

133. Craig, "Did Jesus Rise from the Dead?" 152.

134. Yamauchi, "Easter: Myth, Hallucination, or History?" 4–7.

135. James D. G. Dunn, *The Christ and the Spirit* (Grand Rapids, MI: Eerdmans, 1998), 67–68.

136. C. F. D. Moule, *The Phenomenon of the New Testament* (London: SCM Press, 1967), 13, emphasis in original.

137. Flavius Josephus, "Jewish Antiquities," in *The New Complete*

Works of Josephus, trans. William Whiston (Grand Rapids, MI: Kregel, 1999), 18.63–64, emphasis added. There is great controversy about the authenticity of this text. Kostenberger, Andreas J.; Kellum, L. Scott; Quarles, Charles L. (2009). The Cradle, the Cross, and the Crown: An Introduction to the New Testament, pp. 104-108 is an excellent summary of the controversy.

138. Suetonius, *Vita Nero* 16.11–13.
139. Pliny the Younger, Letters 10.96.1–7.
140. Thomas Arnold, *Christian Life, Its Hopes, Its Fears, and Its Close*, 6th ed. (London: T. Fellowes, 1859), pp. 15-16.
141. Josh McDowell, *Evidence That Demands a Verdict: Historical Evidences for the Christian Faith*, San Bernardino, Calif.: Here's Life Publishers, Page 189.
142. John R. W. Stott, *Basic Christianity* (Grand Rapids, MI: InterVarsity, 1971), 49.
143. C. Truman Davis, "The Crucifixion of Jesus: The Passion of Christ from a Medical Point of View," *Arizona Medicine* (March 1965): 183–87.
144. Richard N. Ostling, "Jesus Christ, Plain and Simple," *Time*, January 10, 1994, 32–33.
145. See Craig, "Did Jesus Rise from the Dead?" 159–60.
146. Maurice Burrell, "Twentieth Century Arianism: An Examination of the Doctrine of the Person of Christ Held by Jehovah's Witnesses," *The Churchman* 80, no. 2 (1966): 134–135, http://archive.churchsociety.org/churchman/documents/Cman_080_2_Burrell.pdf
147. https://www.mkgandhi.org/my_religion/08all_religions.php
148. https://www.youtube.com/watch?time_continue=2&v=owZc3Xq8obk
149. Kenneth L. Woodward, "2000 Years of Jesus," *Newsweek*, March 29, 1999, 54.
150. Ibid., 63.
151. Jaroslav Pelikan, *Jesus through the Centuries: His Place in the History of Culture* (New Haven, CT: Yale University Press, 1999).
152. Stephen Prothero, *American Jesus: How the Son of God Became a National Icon* (New York: Farrar, Straus & Giroux,

2003).

153. https://www.azquotes.com/author/15487-H_G_Wells/tag/jesus

154. Quoted in Woodward, "2000 Years of Jesus," *Newsweek*, 57–58.

155. Prothero, *American Jesus*, 11.

156. Philip Yancey, *The Jesus I Never Knew* (Grand Rapids, MI: Zondervan, 1995), 20.

157. Ibid., 70 from the book *What if Jesus Had Never Been Born?* by Kennedy and Newcombe.

158. Arthur C. Brooks, *Who Really Cares: The Surprising Truth about Compassionate Conservatism* (New York: Basic Books, 2006).]

159. Quoted in Frank Brieaddy, "Philanthropy Expert: Conservatives Are More Generous," Beliefnet.com, (2006).

160. Water, *The Life of Jesus Made Easy*, 33.

161. Kenneth L. Woodward, "2000 Years of Jesus," *Newsweek*, March 29, 1999, 55.

162. As quoted in F. F. Bruce, *The New Testament Documents* (Downers Grove, IL: InterVarsity, 1981), 15.

163. For further study of this issue, the book *Christianity on Trial: Arguments against Anti-Religious Bigotry* by Vincent Carrol and David Shiflett is most helpful.

164. D. James Kennedy and Jerry Newcombe, *What if Jesus Had Never Been Born?*, 225.

165. Ibid.

166. Ibid., 235.

167. John Blanchard, *Whatever Happened to Hell?* (Durham, England: Evangelical Press, 1993), 128.

168. John Milton, *Paradise Lost*, bk. 1, ln. 263.

169. Charles Haddon Spurgeon, "The Final Separation," sermon no. 1234, preached in 1875, The Charles H. Spurgeon Library Version 1 (AGES Digital Library, CD-ROM), 353.

IT'S ALL ABOUT JESUS!